New
Directions in
British
Architecture

NEW DIRECTIONS IN ARCHITECTURE

ROYSTON LANDAU

NEW DIRECTIONS

IN

BRITISH

ARCHITECTURE

GEORGE BRAZILLER　　　　　NEW YORK

The passage from "The Dilemma of Specialization" is reprinted
from *Studies in Philosophy, Politics and Economics*, by F. A. Hayek,
with the permission of Routledge and Kegan Paul, London, ©
1967; the University of Chicago Press, copyright 1967 by the
University of Chicago.

To Nicholas and Francesca

CONTENTS

NEW DIRECTIONS AND
POSSIBLE FUTURES

WHAT do we mean when we talk about "architecture"? Would we recognize a "New Direction" if we saw one? It is easy to neglect delving into such questions if any answer is likely to be complicated or unsatisfactory. However, Jean Tinguely, it may be remembered, was flattered when told that his sculpture was not art, and John Cage was unperturbed by his critics who claimed that his sounds were not music, so may not a new direction in architecture (if it is to be noticed at all) be classified as not architecture?

Architects, especially in the past, have shown a predisposition to calling their own particular interpretation of what they believe to be good building by the name of architecture. But as these interpretations could differ greatly from person to person, and from time to time, the use of the word has become particular and exclusive, so much so that many have tended to avoid the term in order not to be associated with certain of its connotations.

For the purposes of this essay we might define architecture as the constructable end product of the architect, regardless of whether the areas to which he addresses himself are traditional or entirely new. But this raises the question, to which current architectural education is trying to find an answer: what is an architect in this second half of the twentieth century?

Traditionally, the architect was a designer, restricted by the techniques of craftsmen, devising structures for specific needs and using a limited number of materials in a certain range of ways. But invention was always expected of him, although the rules within which he was to operate were clearly laid down and well understood. Only the imbecile or the genius would deviate.

But as society has become larger, more egalitarian, and more complex, thus giving the architect new and more expansive problems to solve, and as science, technology, and industry have made available to him whole new ranges of ways and means, so the rules of the game have lost their stability and their simple definability; the ex-craftsman's designer is faced with a new, multi-variable world in which the old delineations of his activity are no longer applicable.

The effect upon the architect of the accelerating growth of information and knowledge has not been (as some methodologists have assumed) to increase architectural assurance or certainty—to the contrary, it has occasioned an increase in doubt. This is not difficult to understand, for any new increase in knowledge is always accompanied by an increase in the knowledge of our ignorance.[1] We become better and better informed about how ignorant we are.

But the architect's attitude toward the knowledge that he possesses is also influenced by present theories of knowledge. It is now fifty years since Bertrand Russell found knowledge to be based on unprovable principles. He was attempting to show the opposite and was committed to "save" knowledge from the skeptics by giving sure-fire proofs of the axioms (assumptions) upon which a perfected mathematics could be based.[2] He chose mathematics because it is the most exact of the sciences, and intended to extend his program to other less precise areas once he had demonstrated unquestionable proofs. But his program was not to be accomplished, and even mathematics he found to be built on more tentative foundations than he had expected.

With the growth of knowledge and the loss of certainty, the architect might be said to be knowing less and less about more and more, while even what he does know, he is to doubt.

One result of the growth of architectural knowledge has been the articulation of such knowledge into separate categories in which new specializations can develop in detail and in depth. The model for this program has come from the natural sciences which have tended to organize themselves into specialist subjects for the purposes of intense research.

F. A. Hayek has pointed out some of the difficulties in applying the model of the natural sciences to the social sciences, where the intentions of the two areas are basically different.[3] The social sciences, like architecture (which frequently attempts to incorporate findings from the social sciences), rely upon an over-all view in order to understand the nature of their problems and thus how best to deal with them. But the competences required for an over-all view become increasingly difficult to achieve, and the dilemma of specialization is stated by F. A. Hayek when (as a social scientist) he writes:

> None of us can feel but very humble when he reflects what he really ought to know in order to account for even the simplest social process or to be able to give sensible advice on almost any political issue. We are probably so used to this impossibility of knowing what we ideally ought to know that we are rarely fully aware of the magnitude of our shortcomings. In an ideal

world an economist who knows no law, an anthropologist who knows no economics, a psychologist who knows no philosophy, or a historian who does not know almost every subject should be inconceivable; yet the fact is that the limitations of our capacities make such deficiencies the rule.[4]

To the architectural educationalist whose job it is to decide whether educational courses should be oriented toward specialist skills or general approaches, this question is central. Buckminster Fuller has warned that specialization leads to obsolescence (and obsolete activities tend to perpetuate themselves through their inability to see, from a general point of view, that they are no longer relevant); and Norbert Wiener[5] has distinguished the logical structural characteristics of general propositions from the more precise (specialist) inferences in terms of the computer. He has made the case that a machine can be programed to process precise (specialist) data with far greater speed and accuracy than man himself can ever achieve, but man, with his mobility and with his scanning and self-learning machinery (the eye and the brain), is enormously competent at generalizing and hypothesizing, and superior and more economical than any machine. This suggests a man-machine partnership which could eventually come to the aid of the problem of specialization. Mechanization may well supersede specialization. It is less likely to take over the more complex task of generalization.

I come now to the question of the architect and his relationship to his scene, which has been responsible for the way I have presented this text. Ideas grow or develop in a context. At any time and in any context there will be a number (often surprisingly small) of poignant questions (the "live issues") which those in a particular field will find of special interest. The topicality of such questions will be influenced by many factors, which could include: recent successes in answers to similar questions, the needs of the time, the appropriateness to their situation, or perhaps fashion. (Fashion in science may be just as influential as fashion in the arts.)

Radical changes in problem situations will be caused by major shifts of view. In the natural sciences, Thomas Kuhn sees scientists as puzzle-solving animals discovering inconsistencies and errors in their theories which eventually break down and cause a crisis in knowledge, so giving impetus to new discovery.[6] Architectural theoretical positions (the beliefs which determine architectural action) seldom are sufficiently precise for it to be categorically demonstrable that they are in error, but with changes in society the positions become suspect and unsatisfactory, crises occur, and new theoretical positions emerge, bringing with them new ranges of questions and new problem situations.

The "total scene," or the "context," of British architecture is neither simple to define, nor possible to completely describe, for even in the case of one solitary architect, he is likely to have his own network of interests and special set of information antennae, tuned in, perhaps, to Tokyo or Carbondale, Illinois, so making this information exchange network part of his context. Yet the problem of an infinite regression provides the obstacle in the way of any precise account of these sorts of linkages.

My aim here is to concentrate upon the setting in which the architect in Britain lives and works today, although, also for reasons of infinite regression, the picture of the setting will be partial but selective. Thus, I hope, with the benefit of hindsight, to account for certain areas of the past which are now appearing relevant to the present, bearing in mind that as the present preoccupations of architects shift away from the traditional areas, so accounts of past influences must not become confused with, and need not necessarily turn out to be the same as, the well-trodden paths of architectural history.

In the second chapter, the history of the immediate past from World War II to the present includes a series of themes: administration, political decision-making, professional organization, research, regional planning, city planning, and traditional architecture. With the possible exception of politics, architects have been participants in all these areas, which together provide some of the strands in a pattern of usually complementary, but sometimes contradictory, forces.

The live issues in the third chapter represent ideas which are recent to British architecture. What might they tell us about the future? To believe that it would be possible to extrapolate a future from past and present questions would be to express trust in a deterministic theory of history, when even the present (as in music and art) is not necessarily easily recognizable. So, if the present cannot clearly be classified, what authority can the present lend to predicting the future? Present questions may or may not indicate *the* future, but for those who seek such knowledge they can indicate *possible* futures.

THE BRITISH SCENE:
The Logic of a Situation

A N ARCHITECT working in Britain today will find himself existing within a situation which possesses its own logic. It is a logic which has grown out of the past, which constitutes the present, and which will have a strong bearing on the future. He will find himself belonging to a profession or specialist group (depending on how you consider it) which has changed its composition radically since World War II.

That the job of the architect can now be seen to be concerned, among other things, with strategic planning, economic planning, and rationalization of communications and transport is not simply a matter of commitment or even wishful thinking. Central planning of physical amenities has been a committed government concern ever since Lord Reith took office as Minister of Works in Churchill's wartime government and immediately produced a terse policy memorandum, addressed to his colleagues, in five sections and thirty-four short paragraphs, whose third paragraph called for: "Principles of Control and Organization; a central authority responsible for execution of national plan to lay down basic objectives, lay down general principles of planning, to supervise planning, design, finance and execution; regional machinery to apply to national plan and to coordinate and control the work of local authorities."[7]

The importance of this memorandum was that some general ideas on central planning were put together by an incisive and direct administrator in a form which could be translated into action and which therefore politicians and administrators could appreciate. Reith had left the B.B.C. several years before; there he had been its first Director-General and principal administrator from its inception. He came to the Ministry of Works in 1941, during World War II, and was faced with the Barlow Report[8] from which most of the background to his memorandum was derived.

The Barlow Commission had been set up in 1937 by Conservative Prime Minister Neville Chamberlain, with very wide terms of reference, to look into reasons behind the distribution of the industrial population in Britain, to consider what were the social, economic, and strategic disadvantages of concentration in industry and in population, and to report what remedies should be taken in the national interest. It produced a voluminous report, supported by twenty-six volumes of testimony, which principally recommended the development of congested areas, the decentralization and dispersal of industries and industrial population, and the diversification of industrial development throughout the various regions of Great Britain. It proposed new Garden Cities and Garden Suburbs, Satellite Towns and Trading Estates and stressed the importance of the social and amenity aspects of the community and also of industrial and strategic requirements.

If the implications of the Barlow Report were to be recognized, planning in Britain could not be the same after it as before. Here was a formal government report, making a broader interpretation of the scope of planning than ever previously achieved. Social and organizational needs had now been acknowledged, but what was to be the policy for dealing with the situation and how was it to be implemented? These were the questions that split the Commission.

The majority favored action through a central authority, independent of any government department and with a responsibility to advise and to encourage. A minority of the Commission, however, including Sir Patrick Abercrombie and two others, considered that action machinery was a central issue and was being ignored. They therefore prepared a minority report calling for, among other things, a new ministry with powers of control and a capacity for adaptation to changing situations.

The report was published in 1940, a year in which, for historical reasons, questions of peacetime planning may not have seemed top priority. But features of the report were soon to appear in Reith's program, for, besides the memorandum, he was to convene two important committees (the Scott and the Uthwatt)[9] to supplement and to explore certain Barlow findings, while within the government itself he continually pressed for the setting up of Abercrombie Minority Report style machinery.

In 1942, Reith called for a meeting of the L.C.C., City of London, and the six counties around London to propose the preparation of a plan for the Greater London area. His proposals were accepted, as was his nominee for the job of preparing it, Sir Patrick Abercrombie.

London and Abercrombie

The Abercrombie plans for London became the most comprehensive planning proposals that had been made up to that time. They comprised two major studies, the County of London Plan (prepared with J. H. Forshaw) and the Greater London Plan.[10] The first was a detailed study of an area within the County of London boundary, based on principles of land use, decentralization, open space needs, traffic movement, and housing densities. It identified major problem areas, formulated proposals, and discussed realization machinery.

It arrived at the conclusion that, if the recommended standards were to be achieved, there would have to be a large displacement of population away from London itself, and it was the Greater London Plan which proposed where this population overspill should be accommodated.

The suggestions of the Greater London Plan, consistent with the Barlow Report, included satellite suburbs and towns beyond the Green Belt reservation, but its most radical proposal was that, for the largest proportion of the overspill population (a total of five hundred thousand in all), there should be built seven to ten new towns for which sites were recommended. The physical order for the new proposals was derived from the preparatory studies in which the planners recognized "a tendency towards concentric rings of which four can be distinguished."[11] In the report, the rings were formalized and made the basis for the strategic recommendations (*Fig. 1*).

The Abercrombie plans had turned decades of reports and theories into realizable propositions, and Abercrombie and London were to epitomize the first major step in a process of regional organization which still continues to develop.

In 1946, the first postwar planning legislation passed by the new Labour government was the New Towns Act. It followed closely the recommendations of a special study committee set up under Lord Reith, and proposed, for each New Town, the establishment of administrative machinery in the form of independent Development Corporations, having powers to acquire sites and with full responsibility for all planning and development action. Also under the Act, New Town financing was to be the responsibility only of the central government.

Even before the New Town Act became law, Stevenage, which had been a recommended location in the Greater London Plan, began preparing for its new town. At this time, New Towns, of the type being considered, already had behind them a fifty-year-old tradition which had started with the publication, in 1898, of Ebenezer Howard's *To-morrow: A Peaceful Path to Real Reform*.[12]

Ebenezer Howard, in the popular view, was a nineteenth-century utopian visionary, who wished everyone to live in low-density garden suburbs and who hated cities because he felt them to be an "outright evil and affront to nature," to quote Jane Jacobs.[13]

However, this characterization is not only inaccurate but misses the point. Howard did hate the condition of certain cities, as anyone would have who was sensitive to the way in which multitudes of people were living in London at the end of the nineteenth century. (There were low-rise areas of Stepney reputed to have population densities of six hundred persons to the acre.) He therefore addressed

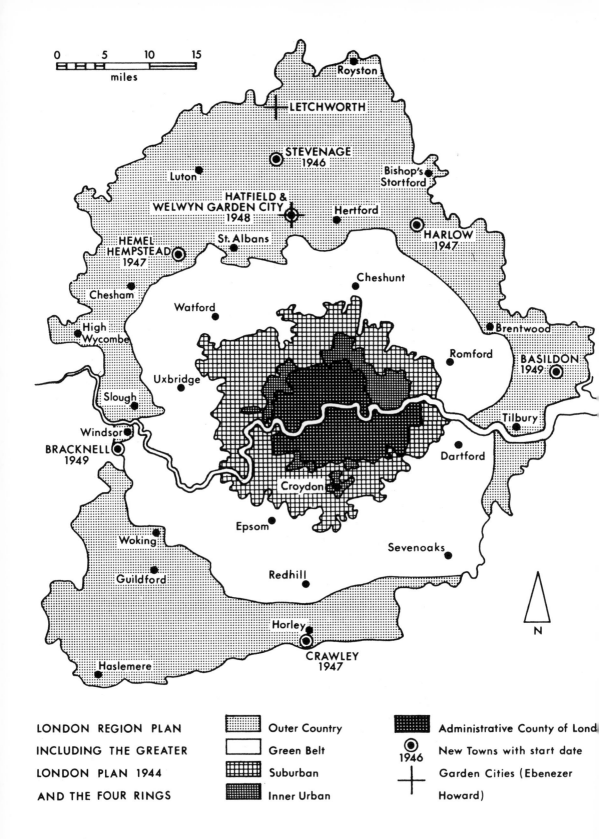

0 5 10 15
miles

Royston

✛LETCHWORTH

⊙ STEVENAGE
1946

Luton

Bishop's
Stortford

HATFIELD &
WELWYN GARDEN CITY
1948

Hertford

⊙ HARLOW
1947

HEMEL
HEMPSTEAD ⊙
1947

St. Albans

Cheshunt

Chesham

Watford

●Brentwood

High
Wycombe

Romford

BASILDON
1949 ⊙

Uxbridge

Slough

Tilbury

Windsor

Dartford

BRACKNELL
1949 ⊙

Croydon

Epsom

Woking

Sevenoaks

Guildford

Redhill

N

Horley

⊙ CRAWLEY
1947

Haslemere

LONDON REGION PLAN

INCLUDING THE GREATER

LONDON PLAN 1944

AND THE FOUR RINGS

Outer Country

Green Belt

Suburban

Inner Urban

⊙
1946

Administrative County of London

New Towns with start date

✛ Garden Cities (Ebenezer

Howard)

1.

himself to the question of what he could do about this. His answer was conceived within the bounds of the possible and took into account the logic of the situation. He recognized that to work within an economic and political framework was as important to success as polemicizing on social good, and that if a convincing case could be made, then action was possible. He therefore prepared his strategic approach, and in so doing stressed the previously unrationalized planning areas of administrative structure and cost analysis which he examined critically as crucial determinants in town planning.[14]

In 1903, his first Garden City was founded at Letchworth, and in 1919 his second, at Welwyn. This enormous achievement, the founding of two important towns, is apt to detract from the far wider issues of why they were there and what they stood for. Howard proposed these projects as pilot schemes for a larger plan which would, eventually, improve over-all standards of living as well as the condition of cities; and forty years later, in the Greater London Plan, Abercrombie adopted Howard's Satellite Town concept, and his depopulation of the city itself, as major features in the 1944 Greater London Plan.

But Howard did not see the Garden City as the only possible way of living, as some of his critics assume, for in the last chapter of his book, entitled "The Future of London," he suggested that the capital's reconstruction had yet to come.

Enormous as his achievement was in establishing his new towns, it can be argued that these towns were responsible for lessening the influence of his theories and for misrepresenting the scope of his intentions. His concern ranged far beyond the town unit itself, and his theory on the growth of towns and the development of new units linked by rapid transit connections (*Fig. 2*) is a sophisticated idea which Dutch planners have used on an extended scale in the Randstad. The fact that Howard's experiments were limited would not have been of such importance had not the first stage of the 1945 town building program been so influenced by an incomplete expression of his larger theory, for the New Towns show the influence of the Letchworth and Welwyn experiments more than an understanding of the whole schemata of Howard himself.

New Towns

From 1945 to 1951, ten New Towns were founded in England. The seven around London formed part of the Greater London proposals and represented a beginning of major planning action on a regional scale. These were Stevenage (1946) (*Fig. 3*); Harlow (1947); Crawley (1947) (*Fig. 4*); Hemel Hempstead (1947); Hatfield & Welwyn Garden City (1948);[15] Basildon (1949) (*Fig. 5*); Bracknell (1949). In addition to the southern towns, Aycliffe (1947) and Peterlee (1948) were founded in the North East and Corby (1950) in the Midlands.

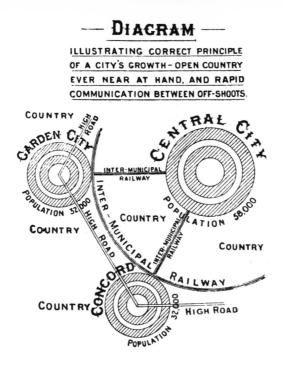

— DIAGRAM —

ILLUSTRATING CORRECT PRINCIPLE
OF A CITY'S GROWTH – OPEN COUNTRY
EVER NEAR AT HAND, AND RAPID
COMMUNICATION BETWEEN OFF-SHOOTS.

2. *Ebenezer Howard's "Correct principle of a city's growth," 1898.*

3. *New Town of Stevenage, 1946. (See Fig. 1.)*

STEVENAGE

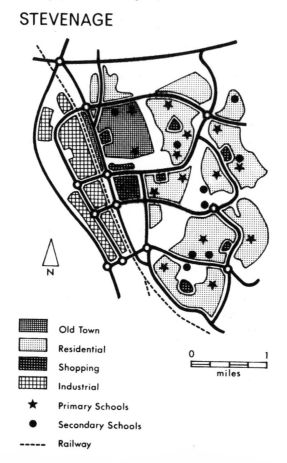

Old Town
Residential
Shopping
Industrial

★ Primary Schools
● Secondary Schools
----- Railway

0   1
miles

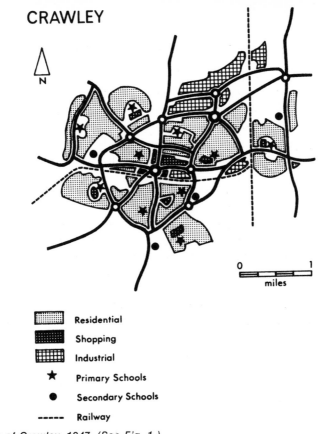

CRAWLEY

N

0   1
miles

Residential

Shopping

Industrial

★ Primary Schools

● Secondary Schools

----- Railway

4. *New Town of Crawley, 1947. (See Fig. 1.)*

5. *New Town of Basildon, 1949. (See Fig. 1.)*

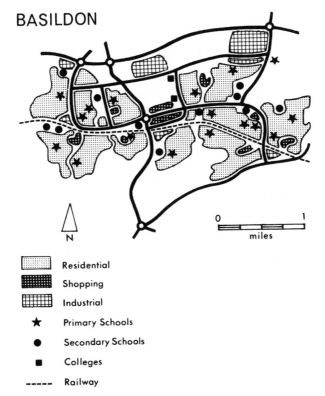

BASILDON

N

0   1
miles

Residential

Shopping

Industrial

★ Primary Schools

● Secondary Schools

■ Colleges

----- Railway

The common components of these so-called Mark I New Towns were:

1. Town Centers.
2. Housing—largely two story—density around thirty persons to the acre—organized in semi-self-contained "neighborhood" units each of approximately ten thousand persons—each unit supporting a small shopping center and primary schools.
3. Industrial Trading Estates usually situated on the perimeter of the town.[16]

The articulations used by Parker and Unwin, the designers of Ebenezer Howard's first town at Letchworth forty years earlier, were substantially the same as those in Mark I New Towns. No new order had been found which might have been more appropriate to the changes that had taken place over a forty-year period which had seen the growth of the automobile industry.

But the fact that the 1945 New Town program, which formed part of a larger regional organizational pattern, could cut its way through political rivalries, a complex legislation, and bureaucratic governmental institutions is, at the very least, impressive. But the machinery with which this was achieved was inflexible and overcomplicated, and, judging by end results, it appears that experimentation and improvisation were not easily able to be realized.

The Mark I New Towns were, to many critical people at that time, a disappointment. Even so well-wishing an admirer of the British town planning movement as Lewis Mumford said of the New Town plans:

A relatively good standardized plan has been an enemy of a more supple, a more varied and imaginative, in short a better form, to say nothing of an ideally conceivable best.[17]

J. M. Richards was less sympathetic when he published his now much-quoted article, "The Failure of New Towns."[18] His criticism included social and economic considerations but was at its most biting when he discussed New Town physical shortcomings, and what he believed a town should be. A town is, he says,

. . . by definition, a built up area, whose role is to provide for a particular mode of living. It is a sociable place, for people who want to live close together, and expresses itself as such through the compactness of the layout, through the sense of the enclosure experienced within it and through being composed of streets. The New Towns, by and large, have none of these attributes. They consist for the most part of scattered two storey dwellings, separated by great spaces. Their inhabitants, instead of feeling themselves secure within an environment devoted to their convenience and pleasure, find themselves marooned in a desert of grass verges and concrete roadways. . . .

To Mumford, his disappointment lay in the manner in which the New Town tradition was being realized, but to Richards it was the concept itself which was at fault. Richards considered that sparse, low-density housing could not provide a town environment at all, and that the New Town dwellings were scarcely an improvement on the "little red roof villa" of the twenties.[19]

A New Town style of architecture had evolved during the late forties to meet the needs of the new housing-based program. It was a consistent style, especially considering the many architects who were responsible for it, and its most standard features were pitched roofs, brick load-bearing walls (often partly rendered on the exterior), painted wood trim, and, sometimes, small balconies. The landscaping was picturesque and usually showed great respect for trees and planting (*Fig. 6*). New Town style housing was Swedish inspired (Banham called it the Swedish retreat from Modern Architecture[20]), but it was also influenced by the official Government "Housing Manuals,"[21] by the minimum conceivable cost limits, by traditional materials and methods of construction, and by a general "making-the-best-of-it" approach to design which the *Architectural Review* called "The New Empiricism."

In retrospect, it can be seen that these were not the only empirical limits to which house builders were subscribing at that time. Under the Temporary Housing program, for example, wartime airplane factories were converting their production lines to the needs of

6. *London County Council Architect's Department: New Town style housing evolved during the late 1940's.*

prefabricated housing, thus giving employment to factory workers in a slowing-down industry, while, at the same time, providing for national home needs (*Fig. 7*).[22] Comparative cost and shortage of materials eventually eliminated the program.

A Dialogue in Architecture

A strong reaction against the making-the-best-of-it psychology, and against the informality and picturesqueness of the New Empiricism, came from Alison and Peter Smithson. In 1949 they won a competition for a school at Hunstanton in Norfolk. This school, completed in 1954, had a formal architectural directness quite new to postwar Britain (*Figs. 8–9*). The 1951 Festival of Britain architecture (*Fig. 10*), which was expected to make a postwar restatement of modern architectural values to the general public, seemed ephemeral and trivial by comparison. The Smithson architecture, strongly rejecting the compromises of the New Empiricism, derived from Mies van der Rohe's Illinois Institute of Technology buildings, although the Smithsons' approach to the expression of materials and to the expression of services, whether pipework, electrical conduits, or ventilation ducts, had an unpretentious (or overpretentious) honesty which extended beyond Mies van der Rohe's own work. Here, at Hunstanton, was a hyper-self-conscious attempt to be antiromantic which earned the school the title, from the *Architectural Review*, of the "most truly modern building in Britain." It became, although in retrospect, the first "New Brutalist" building.

7. *Prefabricating aluminum bungalows, 1946.*

8. *Alison and Peter Smithson: Hunstanton Secondary School, Norfolk, 1954. View from southwest.*

9. *Hunstanton Secondary School Library.*

The New Brutalism,[23] the name given to the antiempirical formal movement of certain young architects of the fifties, is a somewhat misleading title. (James Stirling, who produced one of the crucial buildings of this movement, denies his connection with it.) The name suggests exclusively form-interested movement, and neglects the social concerns of this group which were to be influential in the areas of housing and community patterning.

After Hunstanton, the Smithsons abandoned the Mies van der Rohe vernacular, which leads one to wonder why they had rejected a style within which they had worked so successfully. This seems accountable on at least two levels. First there was an appropriateness in Mies van der Rohe's formalism to this type of problem, as could be seen from the evidence of the Illinois Institute of Technology campus. But secondly, there was a dire need to show a sense of certainty on the problems of the immediate situation in a way that would demonstrate just what the New Empiricism lacked. The Hunstanton formalism demonstrated such an assurance by producing a Mies-aided polemical architectural statement, and revealing, by example, the inadequacies of the much-disliked attitudes.

The early fifties in England was a time when the future of "modern architecture," as distinct from a "Georgian revival archi-

10. *1951 Festival of Britain. Sea and Ships pavilion by Sir Basil Spence viewed from the Dome of Discovery by Ralph Tubbs.*

tecture," was a live issue. The prewar modern architecture of Fry, Connell, Ward & Lucas, Wells Coates, and Lubetkin (founder of the Tecton group), and of the European short-stay visitors, Gropius, Chermayeff, Mendelsohn (to mention only a few), had been deeply convincing to a small minority of people, but had been polemical, controversial, and unacceptably avant-garde to the majority. After the war, a massive national change in political loyalty did not bring with it any noticeable change in architectural allegiance, and, even as late as 1951, a major government-sponsored program for office buildings in London was to be commissioned from architects who were to produce Neo-Georgian buildings.[24] The fact that the Neo-Georgian architecture was influenced by the demands of the Building Code is a historical point which should not be overlooked.[25]

The commercial interests responsible for commissioning new buildings in bombed-out Central London were still largely content with a Neo-Georgian architecture, which commercial architects, and some classically committed architectural offices, were able to produce on request. But work for the private architect in postwar Britain was in short supply, and when it came, even the prewar "masters" produced designs which were disappointingly unimpressive.

The pace was to be set by official building programs run by architect's departments in central government, in local government, or in the New Towns. Certain of these programs were highly successful; for example, the 1945 C. H. Aslin Hertfordshire School program (*Fig. 11*) for 175 schools in 15 years is now a well-known case study in the history of prefabrication. Its aim was to provide, over a short period of time, enough school places for a deluge-rate-of-growth in Hertfordshire. This was to come about as a result of the Greater London Plan's London overspill policy. The Hertfordshire program was to devise a component method for prefabrication,[26] as distinct from the total unit prefabrication method used for the aluminum bungalows mentioned earlier.

The work of the antiempiricist architects was to draw attention to the conflicting priorities of the two principal positions in the architecture of this period. In the Problem tradition of official architecture (derived from the sociological reform traditions of Robert Owen and Ebenezer Howard), the act of creating a physical architecture tended to become only an appendage to the central interest of discovering and defining the problem needs. But the Formal tradition, which belonged to classical architecture (and much of the modern movement), saw the architecture mainly as the object for concern, and the problem only as a matter that needed to be understood as well as possible, and not of a nature to be the central issue.

These positions, which are admittedly oversimplified, were at the center of much of the "is it architecture?" controversy and might be characterized in a twofold way by asking:

1. Does a study of the requirements of an architecture lead to a satisfactory architecture?
2. Does a study of an architecture, taken from the point of view of its formalist consequences, produce a satisfactory architecture?

It is the approach, and the priorities which accompany the approach, which distinguishes these two traditions. The disenchanted younger generation of the fifties was to be prejudiced in favor of the second position, although, after Hunstanton, both the Problem and Formal positions showed increasing awareness of each other, and in the largest, and probably the most important, of the Brutalist buildings, the Park Hill and Hyde Park housing at Sheffield (which will be discussed later), they actually came together.

After World War II, C.I.A.M. (Congrès Internationaux d'Architecture Moderne), which had been founded in 1928 and had become an international forum for the more verbal makers of the modern movement (Le Corbusier, Gropius, Giedion, and Sert), encouraged architectural students and young architects to participate in the Conferences.

11. *Hertfordshire County Council Architect's Department: Pentley Park School, Welwyn, 1951.*

The eighth C.I.A.M. was held at Hoddesdon in England in 1951, in honor of the Festival of Britain, and the ninth at Aix-en-Provence in 1953. At the ninth Conference, the team entrusted with the preparation of the tenth C.I.A.M. included Jacob Bakema, Georges Candilis, R. Gutmann, Aldo van Eyck, and four British architects, John Voelcker, William Howell, and the Smithsons. This group was to call itself Team 10.

Team 10 was to be contributory to the dispute which caused the final breakup of the C.I.A.M. at the Dubrovnik Conference in 1956. The disputed area concerned the Athens Charter, the 1933 cornerstone document of the C.I.A.M., held as beyond the law by the older members but as irrelevant dogma by the younger.

The Athens Charter considered the modern city under the headings of Dwellings, Recreation, Work, Transportation, and Historic Buildings. In certain respects it committed the C.I.A.M. to a particular approach to architecture and planning, i.e., to consider cities in terms of high, widely spaced apartment buildings, and city planning as functional zoning sectors, each sector separated by a green belt. These concepts had come from Le Corbusier, where the green belt aspect had pleased Abercrombie sufficiently for him to have said of it in 1933, "This brings him [Le Corbusier] into line with Ebenezer Howard's Garden City method of extension";[27] and he also suggested at the same time, ". . . between Ebenezer Howard's and Le Corbusier's conceptions there is room for considerable variety of idea, though perhaps the gap between the two is not so wide as one might suppose."[28] That the same young architects found first the Garden City concept, and then the Athens Charter, as ideas similarly unacceptable to them, is oddly supported by Abercrombie's 1933 text.

The Team 10 rebuttal of the Athens Charter framework was not an attempt to show critically why the functional organization approach to cities could not work. It represented more a shifting viewpoint and change of values which supported a Deterministic,[29] sociological approach in place of an abstracted, relational one.

In an unsuccessful competition entry for the Golden Lane Housing Scheme for the City of London (1952), the Smithsons designed a building illustrating their interest in social behavior. This project was seen by them as implying a concept for the "community" which was to be built up at various levels of "association" in an attempt to achieve "identity."[30] The principle of identifying man with his environment was, they claimed, the basis of the Golden Lane project. The levels of association were characterized as the House relative to the Street relative to the District relative to the City. In Golden Lane the existing house-street pattern could no longer produce a socially or physically acceptable environment because the street forms had become obsolete with the increasing motor traffic intensities. The concept was therefore introduced of a multilevel city with residential streets-in-the-air (*Fig. 12*). In the project, the residential route was to be more than simply a link between dwellings, for it was to be a place to meet and a place with street corner junctions (even if the principal excuse for social contact at street corners was to be to empty garbage). The street-in-the-air solution had been used by Le Corbusier at Unité d'Habitation, Marseilles, in 1948 where he had built interior corridor roads; but more similar to the Smithson solution was Le Corbusier's Ilot Insalubre project of 1939 which used an open-sided exterior road (in the north-south block).

In Sheffield in 1957, the street-in-the-air concept was to be used in the vast Park Hill and Hyde Park Housing Scheme (*Figs. 13–14*), by Ivor Smith and Jack Lynn, who were then working for the Sheffield City Architect's Department under Lewis Womersley, the City Architect. Smith and Lynn were of the same generation as, and closely associated with, the Smithsons, and the street-in-the-air concept was a current preoccupation of this group at the Park Hill design stage period in 1953. Jack Lynn, writing on the designing of Park Hill, gives a good example of the then current behavioristic, sociological concern which supported the design concept, when asking:

> . . . Are there sociable and anti-social forms of access to houses? In our zeal to erase the evils arising out of lack of proper water supply, sanitation and ventilation, we had torn down streets of houses which despite their sanitary shortcomings harboured a social structure of friendliness and mutual aid. We had thrown the baby out with the bath water.[31]

This is again a reaction against the popular conception of the Athens Charter and against what might have been done if the New

12. *Alison and Peter Smithson: Street-in-the-air. Competition entry for Golden Lane Housing project, City of London, drawing, 1952.*

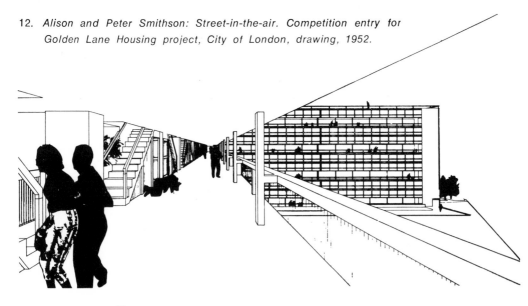

Empiricists had had their way, although, this time, coming from within a local authority (traditionally a stronghold of the Empirical approach).

The design of the Sheffield housing was ingenious and consistent with its theories. The twelve-foot-wide streets-in-the-air (*Fig. 15*) occurred every third floor and always faced the sunless side of the building. As the blocks had been organized in a serpentine pattern, exploiting the views, there was a series of locations where the street changed from one side of the block to the other, thus allowing a "street corner" to occur and a place for vertical service-lift circulation. The streets-in-the-air used to advantage the steep, sloping site so that most levels could return into the roads at one location, thus allowing miniature servicing vehicles (or small electric-motor milk-delivery floats) to drive onto pedestrian streets directly from city roads without using the service lifts.

The pattern of dwelling units at Park Hill and Hyde Park produced a radical and impressive building complex, having a directness and lack of self-consciousness[32] which inclined it toward the Empiricist credo. It was here that Empiricism and Formalism came closest together.

The preoccupation with the concept of "route" continued in the Smithsons' work. In their city center scheme for the Berlin Hauptstadt Competition in 1958 (*Fig. 16*), they proposed, as in Golden Lane, two independent systems of movement: an elevated pedestrian network, built on decks, and a motor vehicle network below, adapted from the existing city pattern. Low-spread buildings on the ground joined the upper and lower levels, and high, independent tower buildings also served both levels and provided reference points or "fixes" for the whole area. The forms for the high tower buildings were discrete and classical; the pedestrian routes, asymmetrical and random.

An adaptation of their Berlin Hauptstadt ideas can be found in the Smithsons' Economist Building Group in St. James's Street, London, the design for which was started in 1960 (*Figs. 17–19*). Here there are three separate, formally classical small buildings: a bank building, a square-plan office tower, and a small, residential tower, all grouped on an asymmetrical pedestrian plaza under which there is a vehicle parking space.

The organization of the pedestrian ways in the South Bank Arts Centre in London, designed by Warren Chalk, Ron Herron, John Attenborough, and Dennis Crompton, under group leader Norma Engleback, in the L.C.C. (later G.L.C.) Architect's Department, has a generic resemblance to the Smithsons' Hauptstadt proposals. This complex (*see Fig. 20*), although not opened to the public until 1967, was first designed in 1960, the same year as the Economist Group.

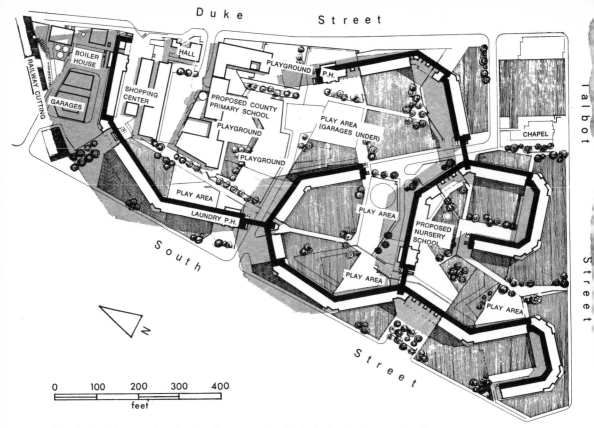

Duke Street

RAILWAY CUTTING

BOILER HOUSE

GARAGES

SHOPPING CENTER

HALL

PLAYGROUND

P.H.

PROPOSED COUNTY PRIMARY SCHOOL

PLAYGROUND

PLAYGROUND

PLAY AREA (GARAGES UNDER)

CHAPEL

Talbot Street

PLAY AREA

LAUNDRY P.H.

PLAY AREA

PROPOSED NURSERY SCHOOL

South

PLAY AREA

PLAY AREA

Street

N

0   100   200   300   400
feet

13. *Sheffield City Architect's Department: Park Hill Development, site plan, 1953–57.*

14. *Park Hill Development, exterior showing elevator and stair towers, and pedestrian bridges.*

15. *Park Hill Development, street-in-the-air.*

16. *Alison and Peter Smithson: Berlin Hauptstadt Competition, plan of central commercial center, 1958.*

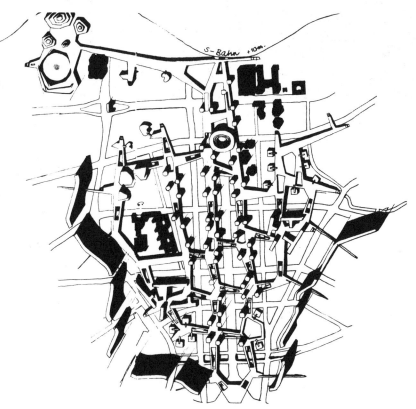

17. *Alison and Peter Smithson: Economist Building Group, view from St. James's Street, London, completed in 1964.*

18. *Economist Building Group, pedestrian plaza.*

19. *Economist Building Group viewed from Bury Street.*

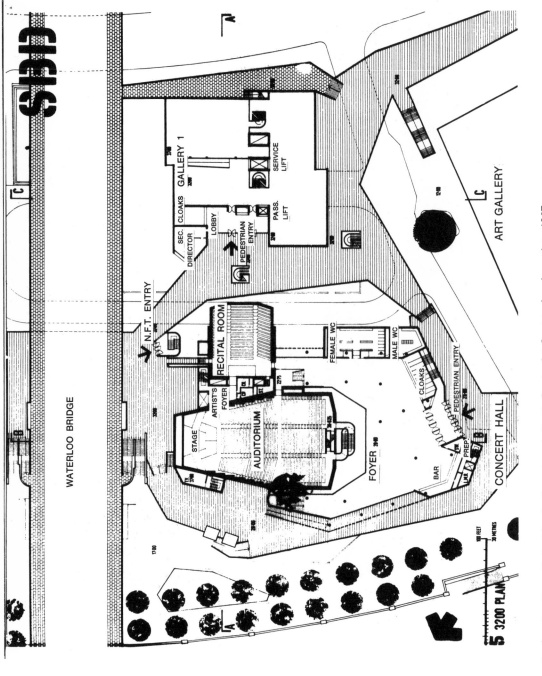

20. *Greater London Council, Architect's Department: South Banks Art Centre, London, plan, 1967.*

Two concert halls (seating 1,100 and 370) and an art gallery are a-formally organized (the "crumbly" aesthetic), and connected by an asymmetrical route pattern similar to that of the Berlin Hauptstadt routes, with funneling walkways through elevated decks and over bridges (*Fig. 21*). Unlike the Hauptstadt, however, the Arts Centre buildings are geometrically consistent with the walkways, both buildings and walkways being formalistically expressionistic.

When Reyner Banham said of Stirling and Gowan, "a degree of dexterity is not necessarily a disadvantage for an architect,"[33] he was making an implication that someone was suggesting that it was. If this implication could be extended to mean that formalistic skill is suspect, it could then be attributed to an English Empiricist attitude, which is perhaps a traditional embodiment of a periodically

21. *South Bank Arts Centre. Queen Elizabeth Hall from the south bank.*

22. *James Stirling and James Gowan: Apartments at Ham Common, London, 1958.*

23. *Apartments at Ham Common, garden side.*

resurging Oliver Cromwell Puritanism. (The Puritans, it might be remembered, were responsible for the destruction of sculpture on the facades of many English cathedrals.)

James Stirling and James Gowan have designed several important buildings in England, which were highly skilled formal exercises showing almost exclusive interest in the logic of the job in hand, and less interest in general theorizing. The apartments at Ham Common (*Figs. 22–23*) (1958), with their exposed concrete from rough-boarded formwork, painted timber, and rough brickwork, became a model of English Brutalism, crystalizing its stylistic language perhaps more than any other single building, but, as mentioned earlier, it was seen by Stirling himself as not belonging to Brutalism at all.

Later, at Leicester University (*Figs. 24–25*) (1963) Stirling and Gowan in their Engineering Laboratories, this time with a new architectural vocabulary of concrete frame, red brick with matching red tile, and aluminum patent-glazing bars, were again to demonstrate that, from a given brief, they were able to produce a building which was organizationally and formally justifiable, which was strikingly original, and which used a vocabulary to suit the job, hence supporting Stirling's earlier claim that his Ham Common language had been only a means to an end, and not part of a movement.

That the skill of Stirling and Gowan did have the effect of giving a Formalist authority to a proliferating Brutalist movement is certain, but their work has also made the point in the Empiricist-Formalist dialogue that no building can simply be the inevitable consequence of the organization of its needs, as the Empiricists suggest; that both the needs, and the forms which respond to the needs, call for high levels of skill; and that high-level formal skill seems to be an even scarcer commodity than high-level organizational talent.

The Public Sector

I have discussed how one of the major influences on architects in Britain has been the Empiricist-Formalist dialectic, represented by the architecture of the New Towns versus the architecture of the Brutalists. Another range of influences of a different genre has resulted from the way in which the architectural profession itself has come to be organized, for the "Public Sector," as the official jargon calls the architectural and planning departments in government and government-sponsored agencies, is large and influential, with scope and resources beyond individual private offices.

In 1938, the percentage of the total number of architects in public offices in Britain was 31 percent.[34] By 1955, the figure reached an all-time high of 45 percent,[35] and the most recent census for 1964 gives a figure of 39 percent.[36]

An indication of the influence of the public sector might be seen

24. *James Stirling and James Gowan: Leicester University Engineering Laboratories, 1963.*

25. *Leicester University Engineering Laboratories, workshop building.*

by considering that nearly all the schools built in Britain, including the programs of Hertfordshire and C.L.A.S.P. (Consortium of Local Authorities Special Programme), the New Towns, the major large-scale housing projects (Sheffield and Roehampton), and most of the comprehensive central area development projects, have been designed from within public office architect's departments, which are annually responsible for about 45 percent of the total national building output.[37]

One developing aspect, for which government agencies have taken a large measure of responsibility, has been that of research. Government-sponsored research into building started on a formal basis in 1921, when the Building Research Station was established. In the prewar years, its main problems were concerned with the strength and performance of traditional materials. Immediately after the war, its problems involved heating, lighting, building-operation processes, and matters of cost. More recently it has been concerned with environmental studies and user requirements. The change in the B.R.S. problems, from simple structurally testable exercises, through pseudo-quantifiable topics such as heating and lighting, to the complexities of environmental studies, reflects the changing concerns during this period.

The shifting viewpoint can also be seen by looking at the newer government departments and other research establishments. In the immediate postwar years, government department research studies were generally prepared by committee. A part-time committee of independent experts would be appointed to make a study and to prepare a report according to specific terms of reference. This study method is still commonly used and suits certain sorts of investigation. An example of such a report is that of the Barlow Commission discussed earlier.

By the fifties, full-time research groups, closer to the "scientific" model of the B.R.S., became more common. The Ministries of Education and, later, Housing set up groups which would not only analyze problems but would also make proposals, sometimes in the form of constructed buildings (as in the case of the Ministry of Education's Wokingham School project)[38] These groups were concerned with research and development work and were to become a prototype for research practices, especially those concerned with building types.

Since the fifties, research groups have been continually increasing their scope and size in the ministries, in universities and in industry, and the body of documented information being produced at a national (as well as at an international) level is extensive.

A recent concern of building research programs has been the comparative inefficiency of the whole building operation compared with other major industrial enterprises. This concern encouraged the

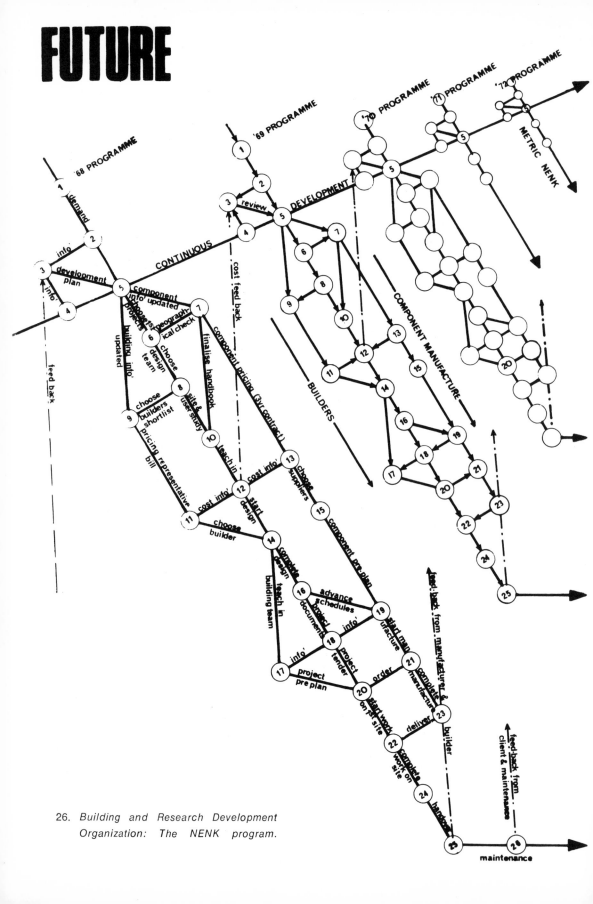

FUTURE

26. *Building and Research Development*
Organization: The NENK program.

government to set up, in 1963, the Building Research and Development Organization, at the Ministry of Public Building and Works, under Sir Donald Gibson. Some principal interests of the organization were in the areas of economic planning, building management, information categorization, dissemination, and feedback; one particular project of the Ministry was in lightweight prefabricated construction. A dry construction, fast fabrication system had been pioneered in the Hertfordshire Schools and was further developed in the C.L.A.S.P. School program.[39]

Using the C.L.A.S.P. program as a point of departure, Ralph Iredale and his team were to develop a system called NENK (*Figs. 26–27*). It uses a two-way-span space deck for floors and ceilings, can be constructed up to four stories high (roof spans up to seventy-six feet), and allows for flexibility in the location of columns. As a total process, it is designed to include a systematic design procedure, a critical path program, the use of standard modular components, a computerized cost-planning method, an economic use of construction labor, and an assembly speed factor. The NENK methodology is perhaps as important as the NENK hardware.

But an increase in the extent of research is also bringing a change in awareness of the potential scope of architectural activity at both the macro and the micro ends of the scale—a scope that is beginning to force architects to choose whether to retreat to specialization (with its inherent danger of unaware obsolescence) or whether to attempt to comprehend and come to terms with a complexity which so far cannot be adequately understood. This is the nature of the dilemma which the information explosion and research revolution is posing.

27. *Ministry of Public Building and Works: The NENK space deck.*

Since 1945 the number of architects employed by Local Government Architect's Departments has never been less than 28 percent of the total architectural profession in Britain. This 28 percent (4,500 architects in 1966) work mainly for town councils or county councils throughout the country. Town Council Architect's Departments, such as that of the Sheffield City Council (which was responsible for the Park Hill Development, mentioned earlier), are largely concerned with providing new housing. County Council Architect's Departments, such as that of the Nottingham County Council, which originated the C.L.A.S.P. program, are principally concerned with schools. The largest single Local Government Architect's Department is in London, and its responsibilities include both schools and housing.

In 1946, Robert Matthew succeeded J. H. Forshaw (who had been Abercrombie's co-author of the County of London Plan) as Chief Architect to the London County Council. The Matthew period at the L.C.C. (1946–53) marks the beginning of an influential and important phase in L.C.C. architecture. L.C.C. Departments, like the Government Civil Service, were traditionally organized along the lines of a hierarchical status relationship, with each level of seniority having control and authority over those immediately below it. Robert Matthew abolished this system for the Architect's Department and, instead, substituted an organization of divisions, each containing design teams, and each of which was largely autonomous.[40] The teams were responsible for their own projects, and controlled them until the job was completed, with the only overriding authority at the level of the divisional head.

The new autonomy appealed to the young postwar generation and especially those with potentially frustratable talents, and even more so because there was a severe shortage of work in private offices.

By a provision in the Housing Act of 1950, the whole scope of local authority housing substantially changed. Up to 1950 the ruling legislation had empowered local authorities to build houses "for the working classes." The new act called for housing for general needs. Housing authorities were now provided with a significantly large and diversified market, which the L.C.C. architects, especially, accepted as a positive opportunity.

Except for the period 1946–52 when the Schools Division of the L.C.C. worked within the discipline of the Hills System[41] of prefabricated construction (also used in Hertfordshire), the L.C.C. did not promote any particular architectural position. Rather, it faced the logic of its own autonomous working team theory, allowing its teams to pursue their own approaches, provided that they were within certain social, economic, and programmatic limits. Conse-

28. *London County Council Architect's Department: Starcross Secondary School, London, 1957.*

29. *London County Council Architect's Department: Garratt Green Secondary School, London, 1956.*

quently, L.C.C. buildings gave an indication of the ideas, interests, and arguments of the time, and in some respects an especially good picture, because not only were the points of view very varied, but also the architects involved included some of the most talented in Britain.

Certain preoccupations can be seen, for example, in the Star-cross Secondary School building (1957), designed by Peter Nicholls and Ron Herron (*Fig. 28*), which was a Modern-Movement, classically grouped building complex with Garches-smooth facades. It had the current vernacular inverted-L window and used a "movement organizing" concourse bridge, an idea of the Brutalists.

The Garratt Green Secondary School (1956), designed by Chris-

30. *London County Council Architect's Department: The Alton Estate, Roehampton, London, 1952–1959. Site plan.*

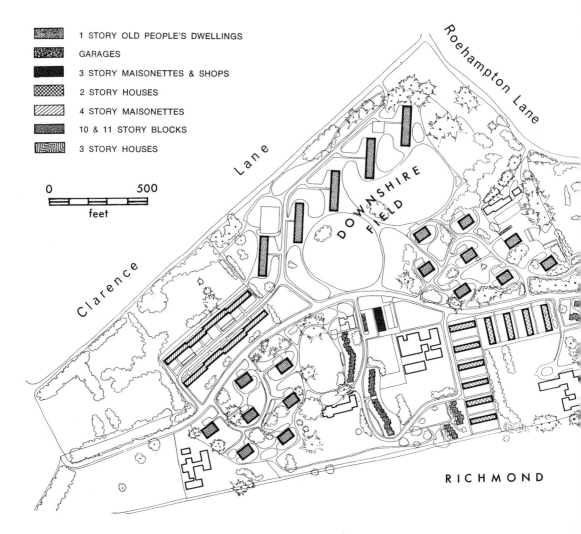

topher Dean, Martin Kenchington, and Ken Jones (*Fig. 29*), was a collection of blocks showing a preoccupation with a movement net and with the "route and place" ideas.

In the early fifties, a major confrontation of doctrine was taking place in the Housing Division of the L.C.C. It was along the familiar lines of Empiricist *vs.* Formalist, soft aesthetic *vs.* hard aesthetic, Swedish-oriented *vs.* Le Corbusier-oriented arguments, and it was represented in perhaps the best known of all the L.C.C. projects—the Alton Estate at Roehampton. Here, on a single site (*Fig. 30*), there was, at the west end, a firmly disciplined, formalistically laid out, Le Corbusier-inspired architecture, and at the east end a picturesque, informally laid out, pitched-roofed, Swedish-inspired style. The

THE L.C.C. ALTON ESTATE ROEHAMPTON

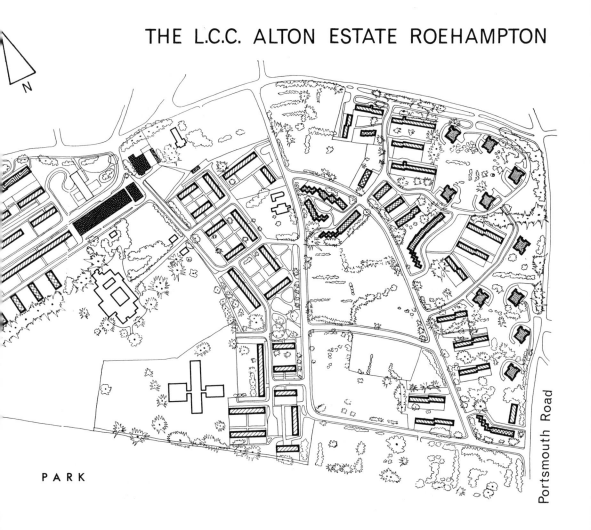

N

PARK

Portsmouth Road

whole site consisted of 130 acres of rolling country with frequent trees and a south side overlooking Richmond Park. The first part of the Estate to be built was at the east end, consequently called Alton East (1952), designed by Michael Powell, Cleeve Barr, Oliver Cox, and Rosemary Stjernstedt. This was the more informal and smaller scheme of the two. It occupied 30 acres and provided 750 dwellings at a higher density than at the west end. Half the accommodation was in 11-story tower blocks (*Fig. 31*), the rest mostly in 4-story maisonettes, but there were also some 2-story row houses.

Alton West (1955) was designed by William Howell, John Partridge, Stanley Amis, and John Killick, under section leader Colin Lucas. It occupied 100 of the total of 130 acres and provided 1,900 dwellings. A third of the accommodation was in 12-story tower blocks (*Fig. 32*), another third in maisonettes, and apart from a small amount of row housing and some old peoples' dwellings, the remainder of

31. *Alton Estate East, tower block.*

the accommodation was in 11-story slab blocks of maisonettes, which had a very distinctive Unité d'Habitation appearance.

The architecture of Alton West used a formal Le Corbusier-derived classical language, was highly disciplined in its detailing, and was consistent in its use of materials. Differing from Alton East, the spaces were positive and calculated, rather than casual and relaxed, and the centerpiece of the whole site, the Alton West Downshire Field, achieved the "grand effect" with extreme success. The most important dwelling type in the Downshire Field backcloth was the comparatively new slab maisonette block (*Fig. 33*). It was developed by the anti-Empiricist group within the L.C.C. and was seen as a new dwelling type providing the possibility of a greater density than the tower block, and a more articulate formalism than the already existing L.C.C. maisonette which was usually only stacked up to four stories.

32. *Alton Estate West, tower block.*

33. *Alton Estate West, slab maisonette blocks.*

The earliest L.C.C. housing scheme using the slab maisonette block was the Loughborough Estate in Lambeth designed by Arthur Baker, Gillian Howell, and Maria Prus. Here, a fifteen-foot frontage was used. In a maisonette concept, space could be most effectively used in a narrow-fronted, deep dwelling unit. So Alan Colquhoun and William Howell designed a twelve-foot-frontage prototype unit which was built and tested and adopted in the Bentham Road Housing Scheme (1955) (*Fig. 34*), designed by Colin St. John Wilson, Peter Carter, and Alan Colquhoun, and also concurrently at Alton West.

The major L.C.C. redevelopment projects of the Roehampton period were "planned mixed development"; that is, with living units in a variety of high-rise and low-rise groupings. The L.C.C. was then to integrate their planning theories more closely into the existing order with their urban renewal projects at such sites as Brandon, Rotherhithe, and Warwick Road. The integration of new and existing, never a strong point at Roehampton, was to become a much more important consideration.

34. *London County Council Architect's Department: Gascoyne Estate, Bentham Road, London, 1955. Slab maisonette block.*

In 1965, the L.C.C. was to undergo a change of function, and, with it, changes in the Architect's Department. This was the result of the Herbert Commission's inquiry into local government in Greater London.[42] The Commission had been appointed by the central government to look into the effectiveness of the local government structure. The greater part of the Commission's time was taken up by planning matters and, in particular, with the question of the administrative machinery for constantly reviewing the Greater London Plan. Reviewing the plan raised two important questions: who would be responsible for initiating reviews, and would the existing administrative machinery provide satisfactory results? It was considered by the Commission that the need for changes would best be understood at (and therefore should originate from) the most local level, but in the existing London local government setup, planning control was in the hands of the central London authority (the L.C.C.) and not the local authorities, which were thought to be too numerous and too small for a satisfactory operation. It was, therefore, recommended that better results would be obtained if the 107 existing local authorities were to be replaced by 33 larger local authorities, each of a size to contain a population of between 200,000 and 300,000. All the new authorities would have both planning and architectural responsibilities, and housing and comprehensive development would be a local, not a central, concern.

The new Greater London Council, whose authority as an administrative unit would now cover an area increased to 600 square miles and contain over 8 million people, would keep an architect's department for very large, or administratively difficult, comprehensive development and also for special housing required by the G.L.C. outside the London area.

Since the recommendations of the Herbert Committee were put into effect in 1965, there have been important operational and efficiency improvements,[43] and two of the most spectacular new projects have been the ex-L.C.C. (now G.L.C.) scheme for Thamesmead, a riverside development started in 1967 for 60,000 people on a 1,300-acre site along 3¼ miles of Thames riverfront between Woolwich and Erith (*Fig. 35*); and the S.F.1. (Steel Frame One) industrialized system, steel frame, reinforced-plastic-clad tower blocks[44] at the G.L.C. Walterton Road Housing Estate in London (*Figs. 36–37*).

Concern for Comprehensiveness

I have discussed certain government sector influences upon the architect, including, first, the information explosion caused by changing attitudes toward research, and then the growing scope, scale, and comprehensiveness in the work of a leading public authority (viz., the L.C.C.).

35. *Greater London Council Architect's Department: Model of Thamesmead, 1967.*

36. *Greater London Council Architect's Department: Walterton Road Housing Estate, London, 1968.*

37. *Walterton Road Housing Estate. Exterior, reinforced-plastic-cladding panel.*

A third influence, without which development programs and public authority work could have little meaning, is the area of planning decision-making in which changing attitudes have raised new questions for the architect, questions which may point to whole new ranges of possibilities.

In 1955, the Scottish New Town of Cumbernauld, fifteen miles from Glasgow, was designated (*Fig. 38*). It was nearly ten years after the first Mark I New Towns had been started, and by now it was much more clearly understood that the earlier plans had made inadequate provision for the motor vehicle, either moving or parked, and had scarcely recognized the relationship between the motor vehicle and the pedestrian—a problem which, in 1929, Clarence Stein and Henry Wright had drawn attention to with their design for Radburn, New Jersey.

Taking into account some of the shortcomings of the Mark I New Towns, Hugh Wilson's design for Cumbernauld abandoned the neighborhood living unit idea and, instead, placed the residential areas around a single town center, such that no living accommodation would be more than a ten-minute walking distance from this center. The housing was to be of a higher density (about seventy-five persons to the acre) than in the Mark I New Towns, and the center was to be reached by a segregated pedestrian network requiring no road crossing. The Town Centre itself (in course of construction at the time of writing) is a multideck building with shopping and other Town Centre amenities on upper levels, and with roads for public transport, service vehicles, private cars, and parking on the ground and lower levels (*Fig. 39*). The Cumbernauld Town Centre road has interchanges at both ends which join distributor ring roads forming part of the town's graded road system. The parking allocation at the center will eventually take five thousand cars. Cumbernauld New Town has been planned for a population of seventy thousand, but if there is a need for a further increase beyond this size, it does not look as if it can easily be accommodated within this particular town organization.

Cumbernauld was the only New Town of this type to be built, but mention should be made of a generically similar (Mark II) New Town for 100,000 people at Hook in Hampshire. It was designed by the L.C.C. for London overspill, but was never constructed for inter-county political reasons. Like Cumbernauld, it was intended to be a compact town. It was to be only one mile wide and to have a comprehensible structure (*Fig. 40*). The densities were to build up toward the center, which was to be multidecked. The preparatory work for Hook and its development, up to the time when it was abandoned, was carefully recorded in a publication[45] which states the premises, principles, methods, and ideas, and consequently indicates the difficulties, of this type of Mark II New Town.

CUMBERNAULD

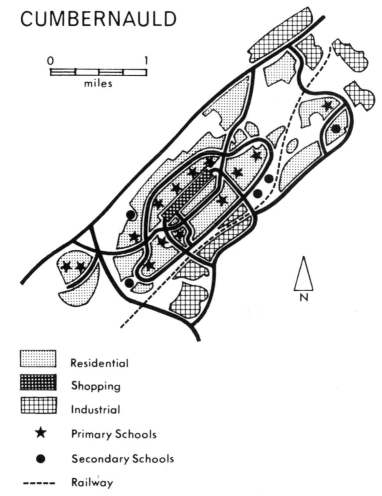

0 _____ 1
miles

▦ Residential

▦ Shopping

▦ Industrial

★ Primary Schools

● Secondary Schools

----- Railway

38. *Hugh Wilson: New Town of Cumbernauld, Scotland, map, 1955.*

39. *Cumbernauld Town Centre. First section completed October, 1966.*
35 penthouses at top.

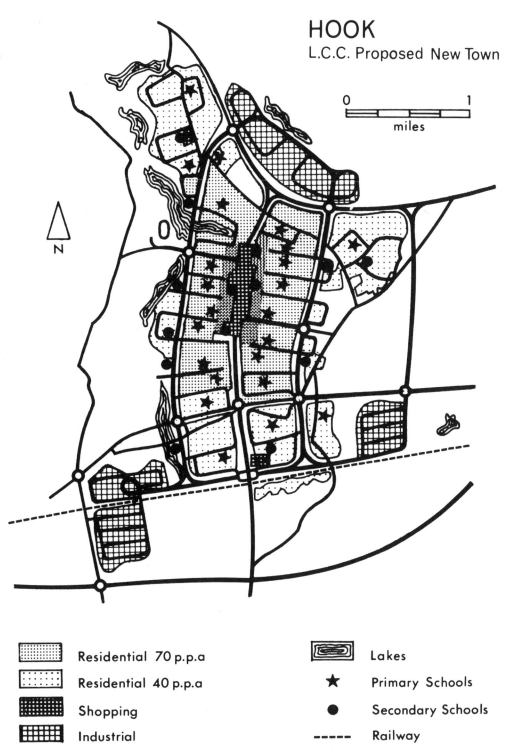

HOOK
L.C.C. Proposed New Town

0   1
miles

N

Residential 70 p.p.a	Lakes
Residential 40 p.p.a	★ Primary Schools
Shopping	● Secondary Schools
Industrial	----- Railway

40. *London County Council Architect's Department: New Town of Hook,*
     Hampshire. Project abandoned in 1960.

Both Cumbernauld and Hook used the motor vehicle as a major determinant in their designs. At the same time, the traffic problem was to be the subject of the influential Buchanan Report,[46] commissioned by and prepared for Ernest Marples, the Minister of Transport, and published in 1963. This report, named "Traffic in Towns," called attention to the possible consequences of a predicted three-fold increase in the number of motor vehicles in Britain by the year 1980. It saw that the "spider web" style street patterns in most British towns were already under strain from traffic movements, and that the larger, higher density new buildings at city cores were creating increasing congestion, delays, and unloading problems, thus producing a generally costly inefficiency. The report considered that town centers could never take the predicted traffic increases with the present patterning, and that ultimately the building organization of towns themselves would have to be redesigned and rebuilt if unrestricted motor vehicle access was wanted. The cost of this operation and the machinery for implementing it were considered in the report, although, at this stage, it was apparent to many[47] that the terms of reference of "Traffic in Towns" were too narrow to form the basis for a nationwide redevelopment program, and that, if the transport question was going to be seen in a national context, a broader base would have to be found. However, the point had been made that the city center as it exists, and even as conceived in Cumbernauld and Hook, belonged to a system of order which was not fully compatible with the full-scale use of the private motor vehicle, and that it was new thinking, rather than plastic surgery, that was required.

Cumbernauld, Hook, and the Buchanan Report were not only the precursors of an increased transportation consciousness in Britain; they also marked an end to the Abercrombie era of determinate master-planning in which problems had largely been seen as discrete studies (of which the problem of London was the largest). The newly developing phase was to take a more comprehensive view of the whole country, whether the study was a regional plan or a local unit.

THE LIVE ISSUES

BY THE mid-fifties it had become clear that Abercrombie's concept of Greater London, as envisaged in his Plan, was not transpiring. He had stated in the 1944 Greater London Plan that "in consonance with national trends, the total population of the area [Greater London] will not increase, but on the contrary will be somewhat reduced."[48] This assumption had misled him into seeing London as a potentially static entity, and to believing that once it had been decongested with the help of Satellite Towns, it would stay that way. The assumption, arrived at from the national predictions of the thirties, was seriously inaccurate, for a large population explosion occurred after World War II, and even more unexpectedly, the rate of increase was nearly sustained. Although Abercrombie's plan to decentralize congested residential areas was taking place, he had not foreseen that Central London would, at the same time, be generating large amounts of new employment (mostly nonindustrial) and that the movement of population to new homes away from that employment would have the effect of increasing the number of daily journeys through Central London, thereby creating road congestion and parking problems, and also placing a heavier load on the public transportation system, portions of which had long ago reached saturation point. Thus, Central London was becoming increasingly, rather than decreasingly, environmentally unsatisfactory, in spite of decentralization, but for reasons not foreseen by Abercrombie.

Although the planning problems to be solved remained the same, the ways of looking at them in the mid-fifties were of a different order and degree of comprehensiveness than in the time of the Greater London Plan, ten years before. A shift of approach saw the new central issue as the economic growth rate for each of the regions of Britain. This changing view had been encouraged by the economic crisis in the North East where the government was very deeply concerned about declining industries, high unemployment, and migration of population to other areas. Movements of population were affecting new settlement areas, as well as evacuated ones, and these migrations needed to be understood if account was to be taken of them in planning solutions.

The attempts at characterizing the regional problems in a broader non-master-plan way began with the South East Study,[49] published in 1964 and prepared by the Ministry of Housing and

Local Government under its chief planner, J. R. James. In the following year, the Department of Economic Affairs took the responsibility for all regional studies, after which time, economic planning and capital investment became prime determinants in the national scale of planning priorities.

The South East Study (*Fig. 41*), like the subsequent Department of Economic Affairs regional studies, made its planning recommendations for the twenty-year period from 1961 to 1981. The physical area for study was defined by standard Census regions, and this method of defining areas was especially useful because the questions to be looked at concerned population figures. The South East population increase was expected to be in the order of 3.5 million[50] by the year 1981, very different from the nil increase for the whole country predicted in 1939. In addition, a further London overspill problem (to the extent of one million) was estimated. What a problem of this size involves can be gauged by measuring it against the 1945 New Town program in the South East. Then, with seven New Towns, it took twenty years to provide new homes for half a million people. The South East Study (and later amendments to it) recommended locations where this new population could be settled, and suggested that new, regional supercities should be built.

The location in the South East suggested as having the potential for the largest of these cities was in the immediate vicinity of Southampton and Portsmouth (which already had a population of three quarters of a million), and after a feasibility study, the recommended ultimate capacity for this area was one and three quarters million.

The Southampton–Portsmouth City[51] was one of the "Sixties Mark III" new major developments, which included Central Lancashire, with a projected population by 1981 of 500,000, three cities with projected 1981 populations of over 200,000, three more over 100,000, and four over 70,000.[52]

The Southampton-Portsmouth study, called the South Hampshire Study[53] and prepared by Colin Buchanan and Partners, is of a generic form which can be taken as including most important ideas of this class of New Towns. It assumes the need for a single integrated coherent urban system to include the two large cities plus the massive new development. This system must be accommodated in a structure which can take a variety of living densities, provide for varying uses, and allow for growth and change. The formal concept chosen to satisfy these needs has been called by the designers a "directional grid" (*Fig. 42*). It is of a wide linear form, as distinguished from the city patterns of either the centripetal form or the conventional grid form. In the South Hampshire Study, there is a hierarchy of six road types contained in the directional grid, ranging from footpaths to turnpikes. The roads are graded according to use,

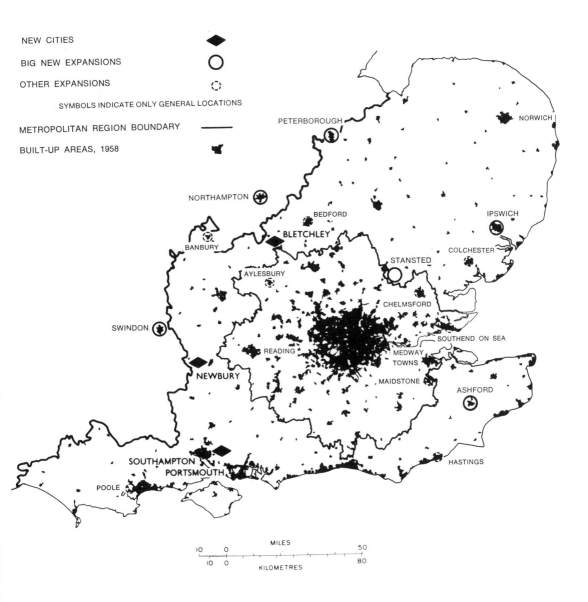

SOUTH EAST ENGLAND
AREAS SUGGESTED FOR EXPANSION

NEW CITIES

BIG NEW EXPANSIONS

OTHER EXPANSIONS

SYMBOLS INDICATE ONLY GENERAL LOCATIONS

METROPOLITAN REGION BOUNDARY

BUILT-UP AREAS, 1958

PETERBOROUGH

NORWICH

NORTHAMPTON

BEDFORD

IPSWICH

BLETCHLEY

BANBURY

STANSTED

COLCHESTER

AYLESBURY

CHELMSFORD

SWINDON

READING

SOUTHEND ON SEA

MEDWAY TOWNS

NEWBURY

MAIDSTONE

ASHFORD

SOUTHAMPTON
PORTSMOUTH

HASTINGS

POOLE

MILES

10   0   50

10   0   80

KILOMETRES

41. *Ministry of Housing and Local Government: Study for South East England, planning recommendations for 1961–1981.*

Residential : low density

: medium density

: high density

Industry

Docks

42. *Colin Buchanan and Partners: Southampton-Portsmouth City, proposed structure from the South Hampshire Study, 1966.*

0 1 2 3 4 5 6 miles

but are selected to provide the sort of servicing needed at a particular location and at a particular time. Until development takes place, roads are not built, but remain as reserved areas upon which leaseholds can be offered for limited-life uses. The grid is designed so that a partial use of the complete system will work effectively, and the ninety-thousand-person living units, for example, at all stages of construction and development, would be serviced by a range of road types offering the largest possible choice for optional uses.

The South Hampshire proposals are intentionally diagrammatic and assume that adaptations and adjustments would probably be necessary when the ideas are sensitively applied to the site at a detailed scale. The proposals in the report are theoretical and general, and suggest an attitude and a type of order.

Land-use proposition

The differences between the Mark III cities and their predecessors are more matters of degree than of fundamental questioning. The Mark III's are organized around the time-honored interpretation of

43. *Lionel March: City Federation alternative building distributions (concentration or linear), plan, 1967.*

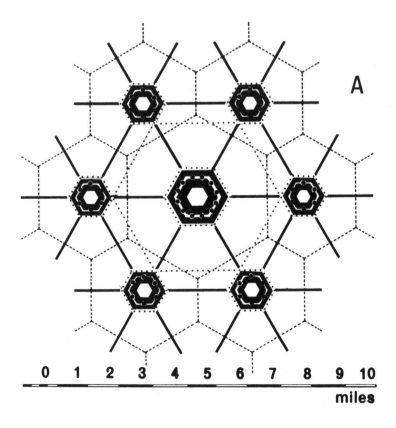

land-use patterning, and with traditional regard for the central government dogma on the separation between Town and Country.[54]

The studies of Lionel March, at the University of Cambridge, take a more fundamental interest in land use and its connection with built form. An example of his line of inquiry is given in his paper, "Homes beyond the fringe."[55] He argues that the traditional form of urban development is in concentrated clusters (blobs) of buildings, linked by transportation connections. A theoretical example of this would be in the version he gives of Ebenezer Howard's city federation (*Fig. 43A*), which was referred to earlier. Town concentrations, judged by present-day needs, are constricted, self-congesting, inflexible, and unexpandable. If the town blobs were to be turned inside out and the same land area which was occupied by the town concentration placed on the connections (lines) (*Fig. 43B*), what

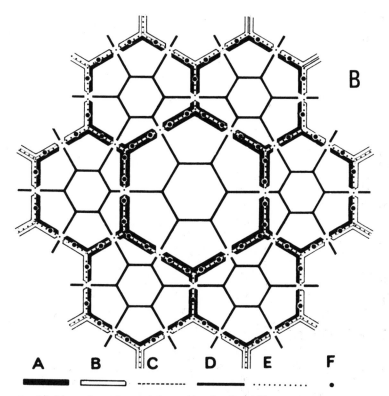

B

A   B   C   D   E   F

A Urban land within city federation
B Urban land in other city federations
C Town administrative boundaries
D Rural main roads
E Public transport system
F Schools

44. *Peter Cook: Plug-in City, section of maximum pressure area, 1964.*

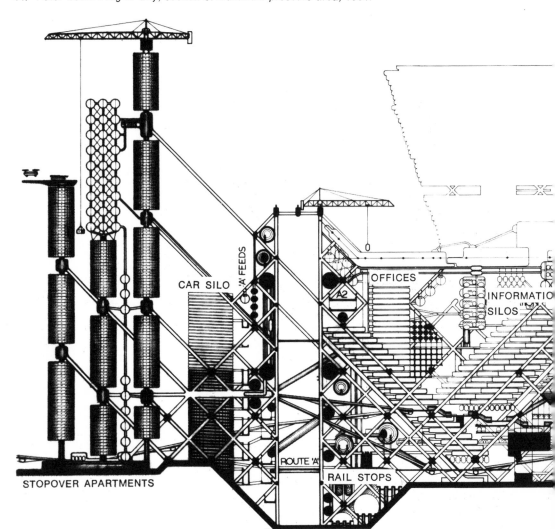

STOPOVER APARTMENTS

CAR SILO

'A' FEEDS

OFFICES

INFORMATION SILOS

A2

ROUTE 'A'

RAIL STOPS

would be the consequences? March compares these systems and shows that linear organizations do not necessarily have the inaccessible amenity problems attributed to them. Their advantages (environmental, transportational, and economic) could provide a new basis for growth without the restrictiveness caused by density patterns of traditional but no longer relevant land-use concepts.

Obsolesence and Plug-in

The questioning of indisputable premises, which formed part of Lionel March's approach, might be considered as one of the most important features in the attitude of a group of young architects whose work began to be noticed at the beginning of the sixties. The Archigram Group (Warren Chalk, Peter Cook, Dennis Crompton, David Greene, Ron Herron, and Michael Webb), who in 1964 produced the Plug-in City, saw the values of their preceding generation as history-oriented and too worn-out to be able to cope with the

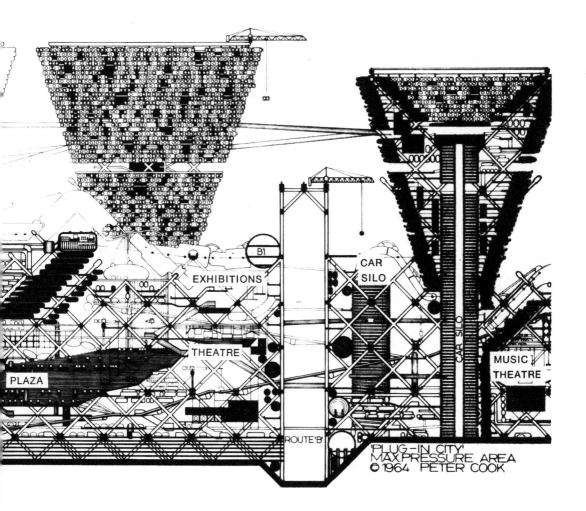

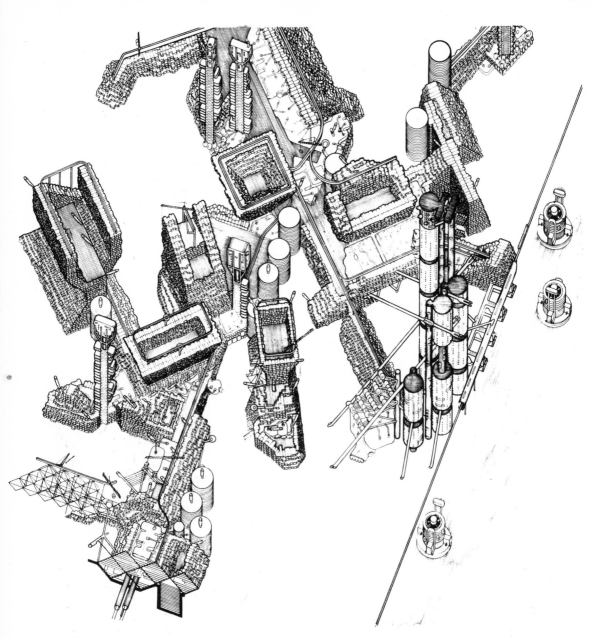

45. *Plug-in City, axonometric projection of local district in medium pressure area.*

changes that were taking place in the world around them. Their approach had been inspired by the example of R. Buckminster Fuller, whose unhampered rationalism gave intellectual credence to those who doubted the way in which unquestioning formalist architects were thinking. A high respect and an enthusiasm for Buckminster Fuller brought with it an inheritance of Fulleresque concerns, such as the optimization of existing resources, the notion of production method as a design factor, the mass-weight question, and the speed of assembly question, to mention only a random few.

But the idea which was to hold an almost governing control over the Archigram Plug-in City project came from that aspect of problem-defining which calls for the necessity, but recognizes an incapacity, to predict far into the future. In the present technological age, with needs changing continuously at an ever-increasing rate, a building, a street, or a city is likely to become obsolescent from a user point of view long before it becomes unsound and in need of physical replacement. The Plug-in City (*Figs. 44–45*) was a concept directed toward this idea. It related the various city components to a time scale in which each component could be given a predicted "useful life," after which it would be economically written off as obsolete and ready for replacement. This was a study in the physical structuring of a system of expendable parts. The question came from the current British context. The solution was a mechanistic concept based on ideas of systems and subsystems (megastructures and components). It is utopian, in the sense that Utopias have always been idealizations of partial solutions, and the Plug-in City encompasses a definably limited number of concerns, but its polemicism becomes most meaningful when seen within the context from which it came— *Archigram* magazine.

Archigram magazine, edited by Peter Cook, was started by the Archigram Group as a "mettlesome" broadsheet[56] to stir up and, whenever possible, to pin-prick the conservative and cautious. It is especially interested in the visible world, a consumer technology, the imagery of technology, and the supporting of new speculative and experimental forms of physical hardware.

Some experimental kinds of formal ordering, contributing to an Archigram hardware imagery, can be seen in Peter Cook's 1964 Exhibition Tower design for the Montreal World's Fair of 1967 (*Figs. 46–47*) prepared for the Taylor Woodrow Construction Company. The tower, eight hundred feet high, contained hotel accommodation, restaurants, entertainment centers with auditoriums, and car parks at the base. Ron Herron's 1964 Walking City (*Figs. 48–49*), which, anatomically speaking, does not walk at all, but retracts its legs and glides along on a cushion of air, possesses both an imagery and an idea calculated to unsettle the nervous.

46. *Peter Cook: Exhibition Tower project, Expo 67, Montreal, model, 1964.*

47. *Exhibition Tower project, plan.*

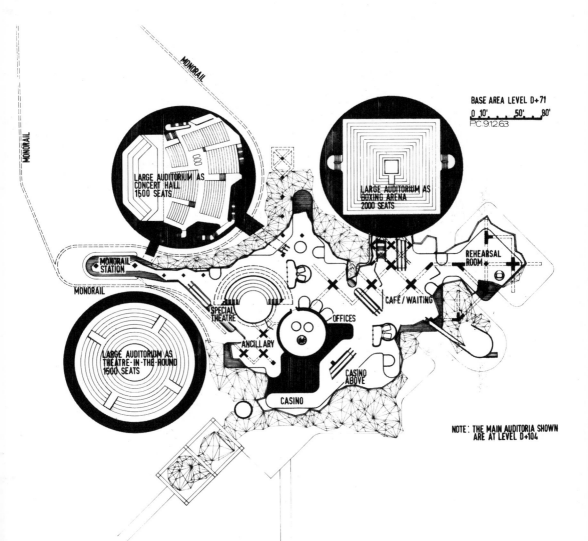

BASE AREA LEVEL D+71

0 10'   50'   80'
P.C. 91263

LARGE AUDITORIUM AS
CONCERT HALL
1500 SEATS

LARGE AUDITORIUM AS
BOXING ARENA
2000 SEATS

MONORAIL

MONORAIL

MONORAIL
STATION

REHEARSAL
ROOM

MONORAIL

CAFÉ / WAITING

SPECIAL
THEATRE

OFFICES

ANCILLARY

LARGE AUDITORIUM AS
THEATRE-IN-THE-ROUND
1500 SEATS

CASINO
ABOVE

CASINO

NOTE: THE MAIN AUDITORIA SHOWN
ARE AT LEVEL D+104

48. *Ron J. Herron: Walking City, drawing, 1964.*

49. *Walking City, montage.*

The attitude of *Archigram* magazine toward indeterminacy can be seen just as much in its format and style as in its contents. *Archigram*s have been produced in different shapes and sizes, sometimes with a pop-up page, sometimes in a polyethylene wrapping, but always on a throw-away quality paper with the cheapest litho printing to match.

The Fun Palace, the Thinkbelt, and Indeterminacy

The idea of an indeterminate architecture has featured as a central interest in much of the work of Cedric Price. He has approached indeterminacy as an idea which can be shown to have a very special appropriateness to a range of architectural questions. In considering

50–54. *Cedric Price: Fun Palace, designed for Joan Littlewood, photo diagrams, 1961.*

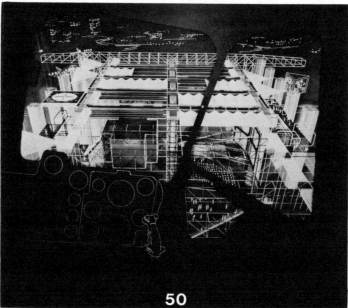

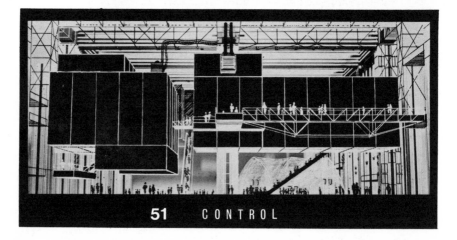

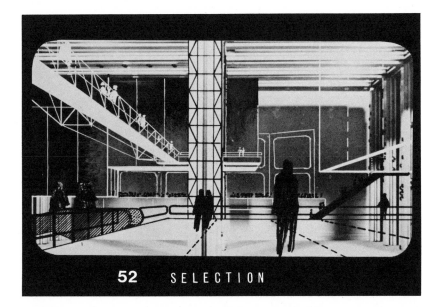

52 SELECTION

53 ASSEMBLY

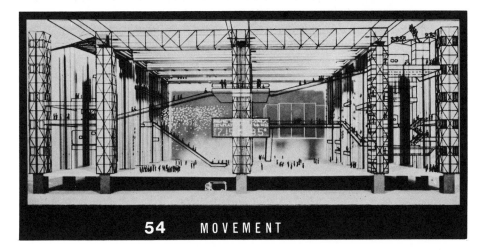

54 MOVEMENT

examples, he has developed proposals always within a very precise and detailed context, so enabling the immediate and future consequences of the proposals to be closely examined.

In Price's work, the connection between the complexities and potential of the question, and the physical (or nonphysical) end product, is very close, and because, like Buckminster Fuller's, his work is consciously problem-solving and possessing almost no arbitrary formal allegiances, the importance of seeing each of his projects as a problem-understanding and question-asking process (besides being a physical or antiphysical, technological or nontechnological, solution) is necessary if it is to be understood.

Cedric Price's Fun Palace project (1961) (*Figs. 50–56*), was designed for Joan Littlewood around her idea for a "laboratory of fun" or a "university of the streets."[57] The object was to provide a place where people could come and be offered many kinds of activities in their leisure time. While not denying the need for routine city parks, the Fun Palace suggests that a greater variety and different range of entertainment might be offered in the second half of the twentieth century than was standard in the eighteenth. The activities which the Fun Palace offered would be short-term and frequently updated, and a sample suggested by Joan Littlewood included a fun arcade, containing some of the mechanical tests and games which psychologists and engineers usually play; a music area, with instruments on loan, recordings for anyone, jam sessions, popular dancing (either formal or spontaneous); a science playground, with lecture/demonstrations, teaching films, closed-circuit T.V.; an acting area for drama therapy (burlesque the boss!); a plastic area for modeling and making things (useful and useless). For those not wishing to take part, there would be quiet zones and also screens showing films or closed-circuit television of local or national happenings.

This program called for an architecture which was informal, flexible, unenclosed, and impermanent; the architecture did not need to be simply a response to the program, but also a means of encouraging its ideas to grow and to develop further. With an open ground-level deck and with multilevel ramps, moving walkways, moving walls, floors, and ceilings, hanging auditoriums, and an overall moving gantry crane (*Fig. 56*), the physical volumes of the spaces could be changed as different usages were adopted. The kit of parts for these operations included charged static vapor barriers, optical barriers, warm air curtains, a fog dispersal plant, and horizontal and vertical lightweight blinds. In the Fun Palace, no part of the fabric would be designed to last for more than ten years, and parts of it for possibly only ten days.

A second major project by Cedric Price involving the question of obsolescence, but this time in connection with higher education, is the Potteries Thinkbelt.[58] It carries his ideas on obsolescence beyond the Fun Palace and into a more complex field where regional planning, national educational policies, and communicational patterning form part of the context, and, as in the Fun Palace, it makes the point that architects have a responsibility to their problems beyond simply providing the architectural hardware. Cedric Price shows that organization and hardware can offer a program new possibilities, just as, conversely, when used inappropriately, they can easily restrict development objectives.

The Potteries Thinkbelt posits a higher educational system, as a part of the national network of higher education facilities, specializing in science and technology. It proposes twenty thousand students for a hundred-square-mile area of the "Potteries" in North Staffordshire (*Fig. 57*), an area which includes the now physically decaying industrial towns[59] once famed for Staffordshire Pottery, but now considerably less wealthy than the neighboring West Midland Region towns. In the study, education is characterized, not as an independent and isolated service for students, but as an industry of national significance, generating here a population of at least forty thousand, and having a major influence on the towns where it is to be located and on the half-million population living in this area.

The importance of being able to accommodate the problem of change with a suitable hardware is basic to the Thinkbelt philosophy, which implies the need for seriously questioning that time-honored attitude to an architectural cornerstone principle which equates design excellence with top-quality long-lasting materials. The short-term solution is not seen by the Thinkbelt scheme as providing a temporary second best to serve only until a permanent "university style" building can replace it.[60] Instead, the short-term program is, in itself, a major design enterprise, needing to exploit the peculiarities of limited time-span needs so that there is no question of straitjacketing a progressive educational policy which expects to be able to respond to constant change. The needs of the educational program, the possibilities offered by the location, and the importance of a low capital investment have each influenced the planning and the architecture of the proposals.

The facilities of the Thinkbelt are dispersed throughout the Pottery Towns and are connected by different communication channels. A channel which has been exploited in a special way is an existing railway network, which is now little used, and is becoming surplus to the national railway needs. The railway reservation links the Pottery Towns and has sidings which offer space for faculty areas. Faculty areas would be of a temporary kind and would be housed on the tracks in a variety of mobile units (*Fig. 58*), thus giving the areas a high capacity for immediate change and adaptation. Heavy,

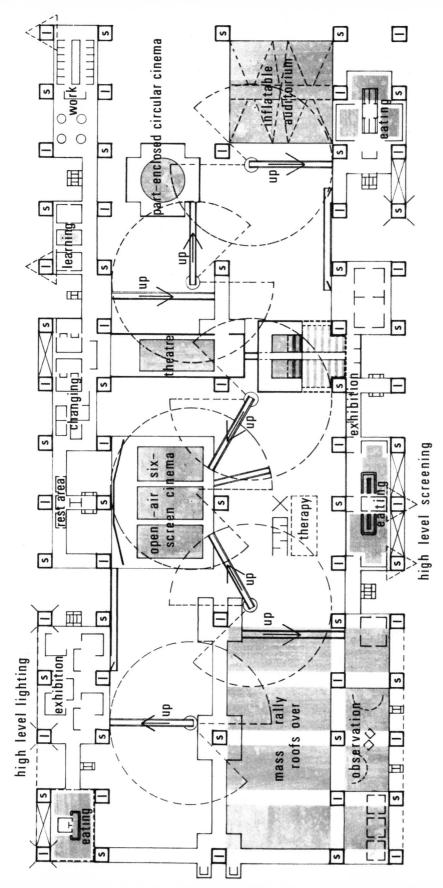

55. *Fun Palace, plan.*

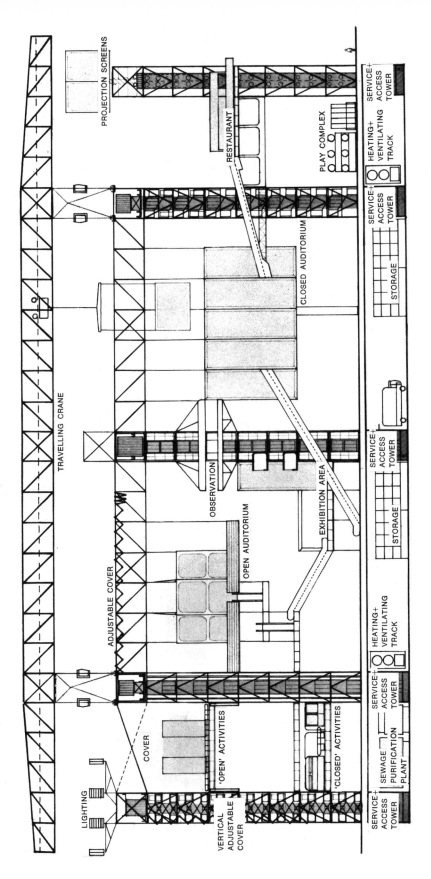

PROJECTION SCREENS

RESTAURANT

PLAY COMPLEX

HEATING+
VENTILATING
TRACK

SERVICE+
ACCESS
TOWER

CLOSED AUDITORIUM

STORAGE

SERVICE+
ACCESS
TOWER

TRAVELLING CRANE

ADJUSTABLE COVER

OBSERVATION

OPEN AUDITORIUM

EXHIBITION AREA

SERVICE+
ACCESS
TOWER

STORAGE

HEATING+
VENTILATING
TRACK

COVER

LIGHTING

'OPEN' ACTIVITIES

'CLOSED' ACTIVITIES

VERTICAL
ADJUSTABLE
COVER

SERVICE+
ACCESS
TOWER

SEWAGE
PURIFICATION
PLANT

SERVICE+
ACCESS
TOWER

56. *Fun Palace, section of an early scheme. There have been service and structural modifications since this version.*

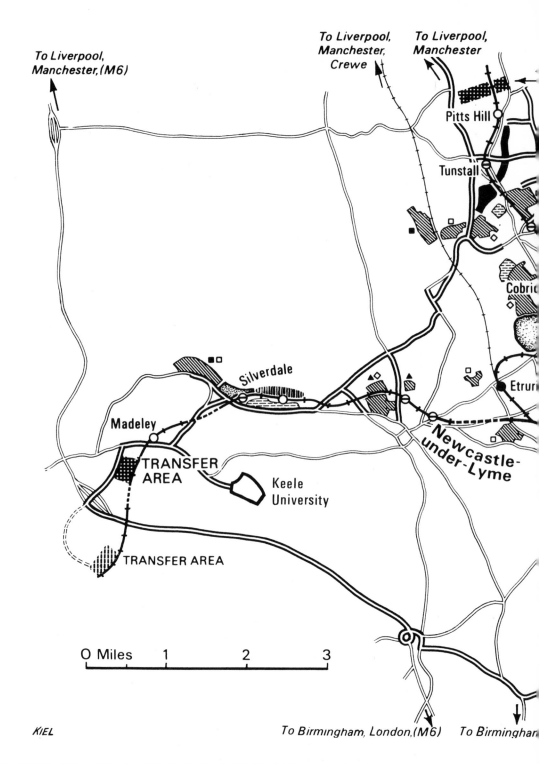

To Liverpool, Manchester, (M6)

To Liverpool, Manchester, Crewe

To Liverpool, Manchester

Pitts Hill

Tunstall

Cobri

Silverdale

Etrur

Madeley

Newcastle-under-Lyme

TRANSFER AREA

Keele University

TRANSFER AREA

O Miles   1   2   3

KIEL

To Birmingham, London, (M6)   To Birmingham

57. *Cedric Price: Potteries Thinkbelt, North Staffordshire, map showing routes, faculty areas, transfer areas, and housing.*

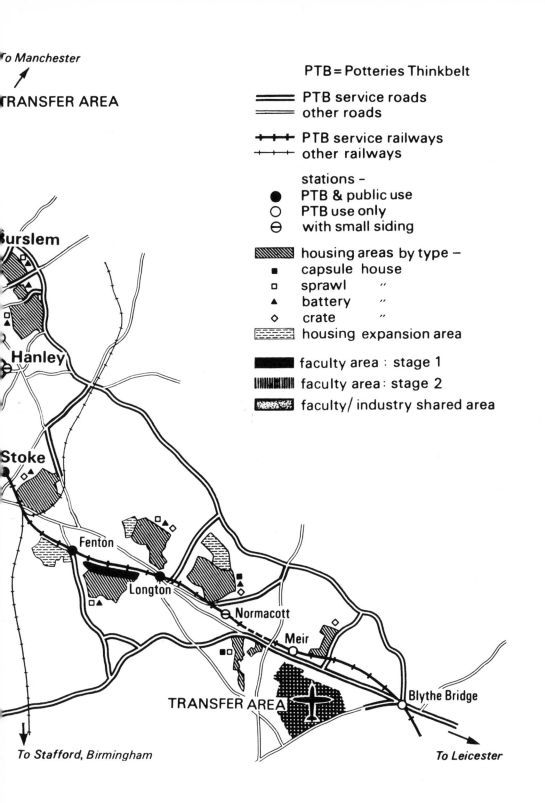

To Manchester

TRANSFER AREA

PTB = Potteries Thinkbelt

═══ PTB service roads
═══ other roads

┿┿┿ PTB service railways
┼┼┼ other railways

stations –
● PTB & public use
○ PTB use only
⊖ with small siding

▨ housing areas by type –
■ capsule house
□ sprawl   "
▲ battery   "
◇ crate   "
▤ housing expansion area

■ faculty area : stage 1
▥ faculty area : stage 2
▨ faculty/ industry shared area

Burslem

Hanley

Stoke

Fenton

Longton

Normacott

Meir

Blythe Bridge

TRANSFER AREA

To Stafford, Birmingham

To Leicester

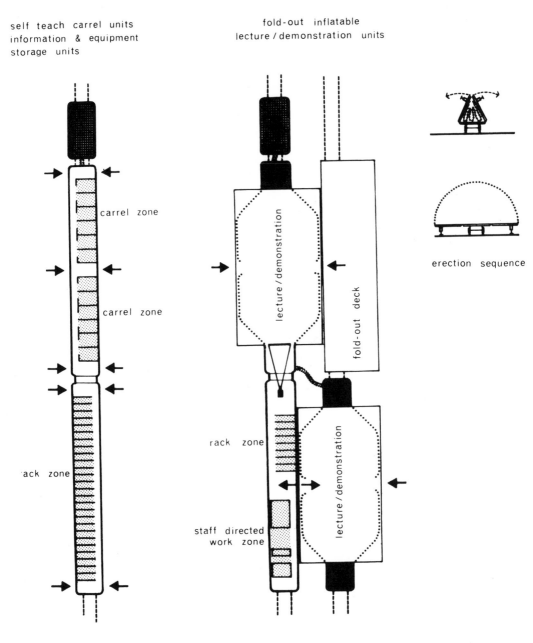

self teach carrel units
information & equipment
storage units

fold-out inflatable
lecture/demonstration units

carrel zone

carrel zone

ack zone

rack zone

lecture/demonstration

fold-out deck

rack zone

staff directed
work zone

lecture/demonstration

erection sequence

STATIC BUT MOVABL

58. *Potteries Thinkbelt. Plan of faculty area rail-based teaching-learning
units.*

specialized or fine control enclosures
sited on fold-out decking units

typical condition at small existing siding
with carrel units linked to televised
lecture/demonstration by closed circuit
or open transmission: ramp access

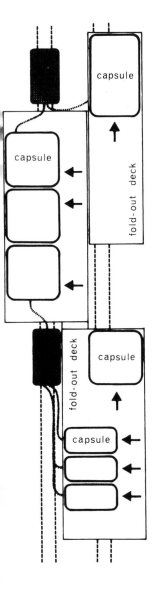

capsule

capsule

fold-out deck

fold-out deck

capsule

capsule

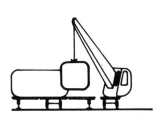

handling by travelling crane

------------- railway track

.... inflatable

services boost or
motive power unit

less impermanent laboratory and experimental plants would be sited at reservations (*Figs. 59–60*) on the three extremities of the area, where people, goods, and plant would transfer from in and out of the network, using local road or Thinkbelt rail services, national road, or rail links, or the Thinkbelt airstrip. A Thinkbelt railbus service would not, in any way, exclude the use of private cars or any other forms of transportation and, as student car-ownership increased (coinciding with the growth of the Thinkbelt), so pressure on the railbus service would change. Also, as learning through information-transfer equipment developed, so the need for physical movements would be reduced.

The anti-isolated-learning-community view taken by the Thinkbelt carries with it an anti-dormitory corollary. Student housing becomes an integral part of local authority housing where, because of

59. *Potteries Thinkbelt. One of the three transfer areas. Montage drawing of the Madeley transfer area.*

its three-to-five-year student resident cycle, it is seen as offering an opportunity for researching into possible new ways of living, with new types of housing.

Energy Planning

The idea of an architecture which will encourage and improve the efficiency of the activity it houses, and yet restrict it to a very minimum, is analogous to the physical concept of a machine which has an input and an energy output, and whose efficiency can be measured by the manner in which it smoothly converts input to output, with the minimum of energy irretrievably lost (entropy). Living organisms are machines with input and output continuously exchanging energies with the environment in a perfectly balanced and regenerative way, and the physical concept of the efficient energy

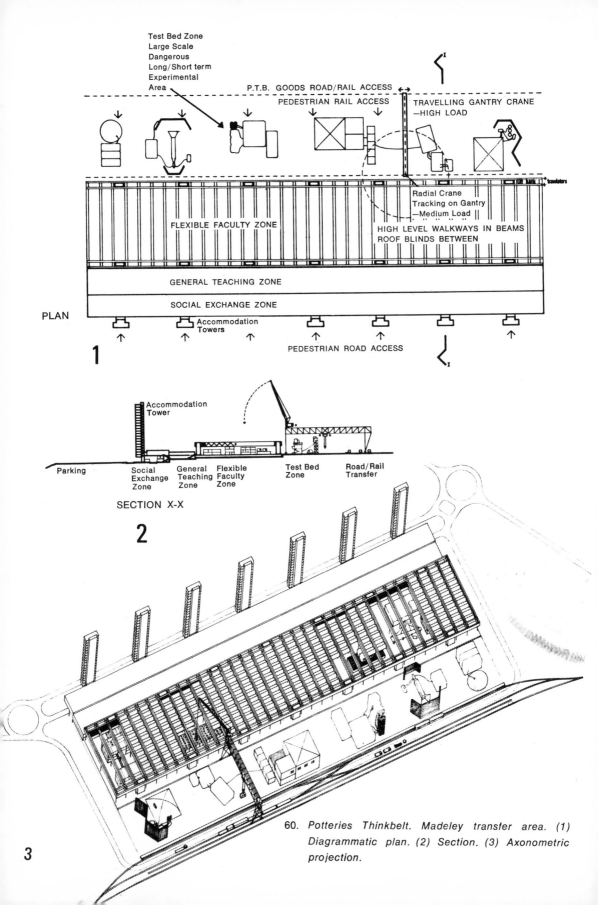

Test Bed Zone
Large Scale
Dangerous
Long/Short term
Experimental
Area

P.T.B. GOODS ROAD/RAIL ACCESS

PEDESTRIAN RAIL ACCESS

TRAVELLING GANTRY CRANE
—HIGH LOAD

FLEXIBLE FACULTY ZONE

Radial Crane
Tracking on Gantry
—Medium Load

HIGH LEVEL WALKWAYS IN BEAMS
ROOF BLINDS BETWEEN

PLAN

GENERAL TEACHING ZONE

SOCIAL EXCHANGE ZONE

Accommodation
Towers

PEDESTRIAN ROAD ACCESS

1

Accommodation
Tower

Parking

Social
Exchange
Zone

General
Teaching
Zone

Flexible
Faculty
Zone

Test Bed
Zone

Road/Rail
Transfer

SECTION X-X

2

3

60. *Potteries Thinkbelt. Madeley transfer area. (1)
Diagrammatic plan. (2) Section. (3) Axonometric
projection.*

use of a system, with the added ecological refinement of a regenerating, balanced environment, form two of the issues central to Robert Drew's regional planning thesis.

Seen from an "energy potential" point of view, changes throughout history, from primitive man up to the present time, can be accounted for by those discoveries which have led to the production of higher "energy surpluses" for their societies, and large "energy surplus" increases have been responsible for radical changes in the economic, social, and physical structures of the societies in which they have occurred.[61] The richer, twentieth-century "high-energy" societies use great amounts of their national capacities producing energy, and yet a large part of this paid-for energy is thrown away through poor exploitation rather than through calculated waste (which is a feature of a high-energy society).

In his Solway Project,[62] Robert Drew examines the development possibilities of an area around the Solway Firth (the border location on the west coast where England adjoins Scotland), especially with regard to the potential offered by the expanses of water, the suitability of the area for energy generation, and its capacity for meeting future communicational needs. He shows that by closely integrating these three factors a regional policy can be arrived at which, by exploiting energy conversion, would permit energy to be used at a level of efficiency approaching 90 percent (33 percent is nearer normal). This would be achieved by generating the sixty thousand megawatts, which it is estimated that this region, with its proposed barrage, could reasonably take, not in conventional "electricity only" power stations, but in Project Power Centres. A present-day natural uranium-magnox reactor has an energy output of approximately one-third electricity and two-thirds low-grade heat. The unutilized low-grade heat from British power stations amounts to an annual energy equivalent of 120 twenty-five-thousand-ton oil tankers. The Project Power Centres, therefore, would become part of an integrated development operation in which the power station surpluses would be used in a waste consuming process, so that steam, hot water, and irradiation facilities would be available to the region as part of a development package. This would give the development area a whole new range of agricultural, horticultural, fish farming, district space-heating, and industrial irradiation possibilities.

The same energy conservation principle is now also being used, on a different scale, for developing "total energy" systems. "Total energy" systems are miniaturized local power supplies which, in a British version first developed by the National Research Development Corporation, can convert piped natural gas into electrical energy at an efficiency of up to 80 percent by the use of a fuel cell (electrochemical device).

A No-building Laboratory

A recent testing laboratory (*Fig. 61*) completed in 1966, which uses the "full integration of problem with environment" principle in an ingenious way, is the National Tower Testing Station, in Cheddar, Somerset, built and owned by the Central Electricity Generating Board and operated as a commercial testing laboratory.

Although quite unconnected with any recent architectural theorizing, it is a classic anti-building in the best Cedric Price tradition. It was designed by a team under W. R. Box of the Central Electricity Generating Board as a facility for the full-scale testing of electrical transmission towers and other types of structures. W. R. Box's program was for a station with a limited twenty-five-year life, capable of simulating environments of probable ranges of tower structures to be expected during this time.

61. *W. R. Box and team: Central Electricity Generating Board's National Tower Testing Station at Cheddar, Somerset, 1966.*

The testing laboratory program called for a mounting pad of one hundred feet square onto which the structure could be anchored, and which would take vertical load points, plus two elevated loading points at a height of two hundred feet above the pad, so placed that all loads could be resolved in a segment of ninety degrees. The loading points would use highly exacting (one percent maximum error at full load) hydraulic rams in conjunction with a closed loop servo system which allows loading to be regulated in a precise proportion (*Fig. 62*). To achieve these conditions in a built structure which would have to be over two hundred feet high, would involve excessive costs and would not be as full of possibilities as the chosen abandoned-quarry solution. The Cheddar quarry (*Fig. 63*) was able to provide two cliff faces, two hundred feet high and at right angles to one another, and the necessary floor area, with rock

62. *National Tower Testing Station.*

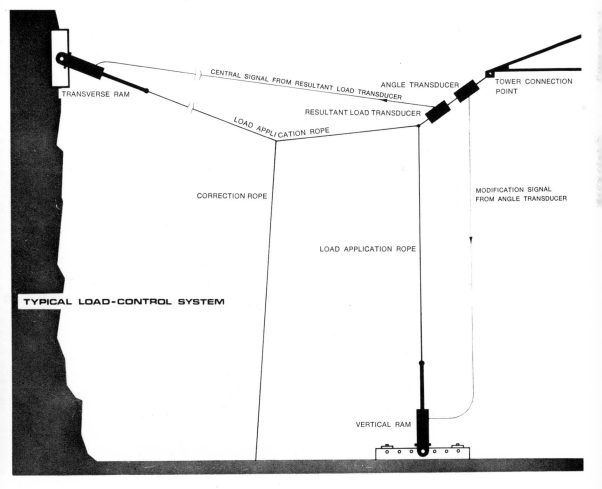

TRANSVERSE RAM

CENTRAL SIGNAL FROM RESULTANT LOAD TRANSDUCER

ANGLE TRANSDUCER

TOWER CONNECTION POINT

RESULTANT LOAD TRANSDUCER

LOAD APPLICATION ROPE

CORRECTION ROPE

MODIFICATION SIGNAL FROM ANGLE TRANSDUCER

LOAD APPLICATION ROPE

TYPICAL LOAD-CONTROL SYSTEM

VERTICAL RAM

faces of suitable compaction. The location gave reasonable physical access, and good links with the required servicing needs. The quarry concept produced a laboratory with a continually increasing facility. Each new test situation could necessitate the use of the rock faces in a new way, thus increasing the equipment and the scope of the laboratory. If required, the quarry could be roofed over for bad weather or round-the-clock testing, and it is of such a nature that it can be adapted, adjusted, and, when no longer needed, just abandoned without affecting the countryside, for the low initial investment of £400,000 encourages an exploitable and expendable attitude toward it.

Thoughts on Habitation

Some fundamental questioning of shelter and habitational needs has been responsible for certain new design propositions which, although sometimes showing a tendency toward being self-contained exercises, are nevertheless posing promising new questions and raising new doubts in an area where traditions and prejudice are still very strong.

One proposition, the capsule concept, now an international pre-occupation (Buckminster Fuller, Ionel Schein, the Metabolists of Japan) recognizes the new possibilities of industrial fabrication, and attempts to propose a complete factory-fabricated unit, capable of economic production, and both transportable and compact.

Warren Chalk's Plug-in capsule-unit Circular Tower (1964) (*Fig. 64*) uses units which can be replaced by new, improved versions as

63. *National Tower Testing Station, photo diagram.*

TRANSVERSE RAM STATION

LONGITUDINAL RAM STATION

CONTROL ROOM

MOUNTING PAD

HYDRAULIC-PUMP HOUSE

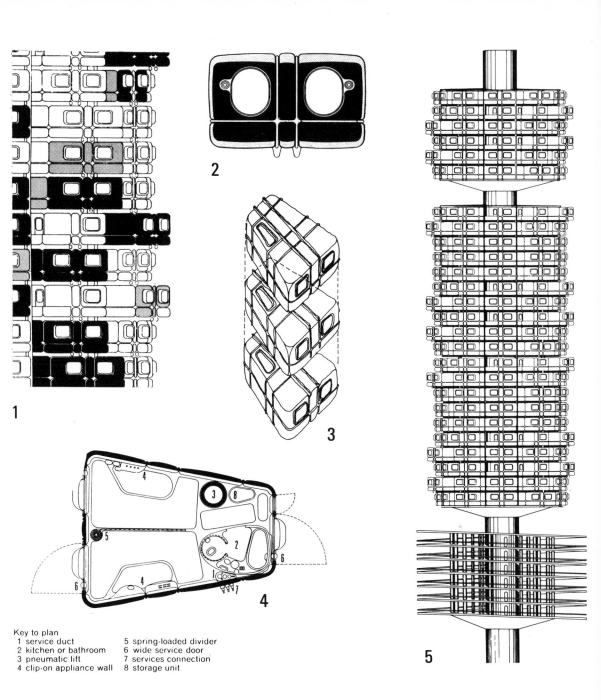

1

2

3

4

5

Key to plan
1 service duct
2 kitchen or bathroom
3 pneumatic lift
4 clip-on appliance wall
5 spring-loaded divider
6 wide service door
7 services connection
8 storage unit

64. *Warren Chalk: Plug-in living-unit Circular Tower, 1964. (1) Detail of tower. (2) Capsule-exterior face. (3) Axonometric projection of capsules. (4) Plan of capsule (see key). (5) Elevation of tower.*

they become available. Within it, the capsule contains a clip-on appliance wall, which can be changed more frequently (and at different time intervals) than the capsule itself. A different capsule arrangement by Ron Herron and Warren Chalk, the Gasket Capsule (1965) (*Fig. 65*) provides for a horizontal servicing of the capsules along a feeder umbilical cord.

A capsule concept is used by Terence Farrell and Nicholas Grimshaw in a recently completed bathroom tower structure in Paddington, London (*Fig. 66*), where a series of identical reinforced plastic capsule bathroom units are set into a spiral ramp tower which connects into, and provides the washing facilities for, a new dormitory building which has been converted from six adjoining row houses.

The capsule as a lightweight mobile unit, set onto the ground and moved around as needed (trailers meet this definition), is being used by the G.L.C. in their transportable house program (*Fig. 67*). Their units have been constructed for an expected life of from sixteen to twenty years.

A capsule as a small office building, thirty-eight feet long, twenty-three feet wide, and nineteen feet high was made in 1963

65. *Ron J. Herron and Warren Chalk: The Gasket Capsule, 1965.*

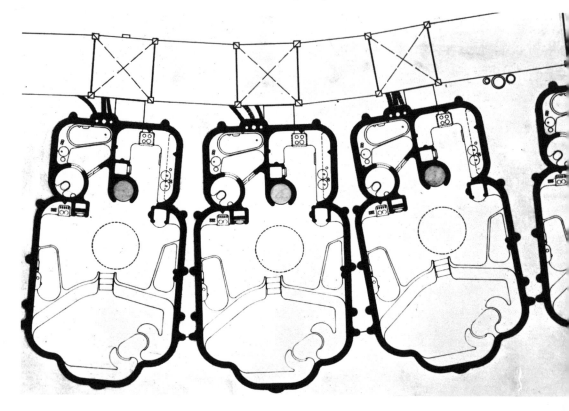

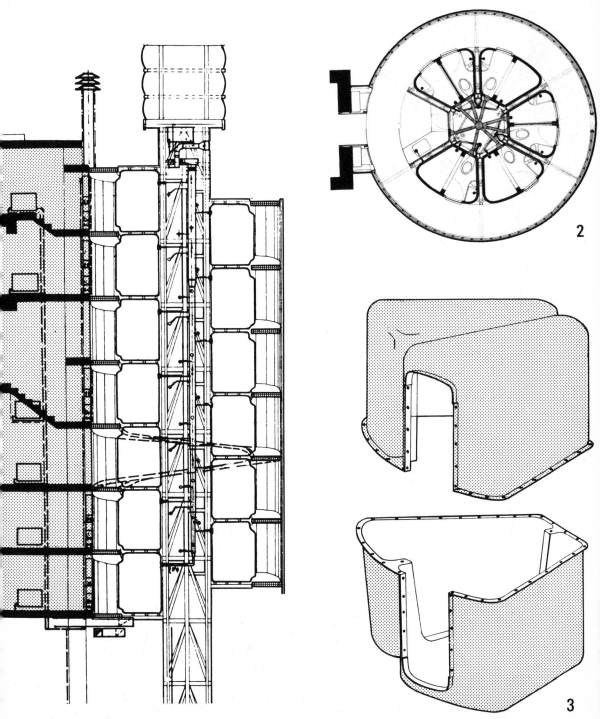

66. *Terence Farrell and Nicholas Grimshaw: Bathroom Tower, London, 1967. (1) Section through tower. (2) Plan. (3) Reinforced plastic bathroom capsule.*

from reinforced plastic by Mickleover of London for the Bakelite Company in Birmingham (*Fig. 68*). This is similar to two portable buildings made by them for use in the Antarctic.

The capsule in its purest form is a die-stamped dwelling which is highly particularized and therefore inflexible. A living unit concept which is the opposite of this (being universal and thus highly flexible) is found in Cedric Price's Battery Housing (one of the four housing types in the Thinkbelt). The Battery Housing (*Fig. 69*) gives a sealed environment, fully serviced from floor and ceiling truss spaces, thus providing a network of service locations gridded uniformly over the whole universal space. The space can be divided up into units by soundproof nonloadbearing partitions which can be relocated as required.

Michael Webb and David Greene's Drive-in Housing (1966)[63] takes, as a starting point, a car-mobilized community in which the

67. *Greater London Council: Mobile home.*

car is more than simply a means of transportation (e.g., as in a drive-in cinema or a drive-in restaurant). A standard drive-in system has two principal component parts—a servicing unit supplying the needs and a consumer unit (the car) providing the space. In applying this articulation to housing, Webb and Greene propose an immobile service unit (kitchen, bathroom, dressing area) to contain heavy, bulky equipment, and mobile vehicle living units built with a folding panel system for enlargement, adaptation, division, or joining up with other units to produce larger spaces when required. This concept has been applied to Plug-in-type frame structures (*Fig. 70*), and on the ground. In the ground level example, the Drive-in Housing project suggests that, for economy of space, the service units, when grouped together, should be hydraulically expandable or contractable (*Fig. 71*), depending upon the number of mobile living units being serviced by them at one time.

68. *Mickleover of London: Two-story reinforced plastic structure, Birmingham, 1963.*

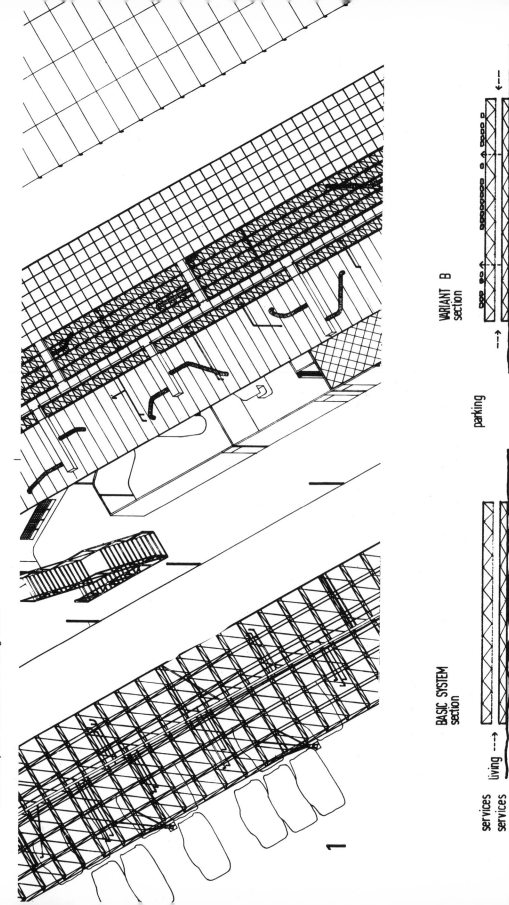

69. Cedric Price: Battery Housing for the Thinkbelt, 1965. (1) Cut-away axonometric projection showing construction and services. (2) Sections and plan variations at living level.

BASIC SYSTEM
section

services

services

living →

parking

VARIANT B
section

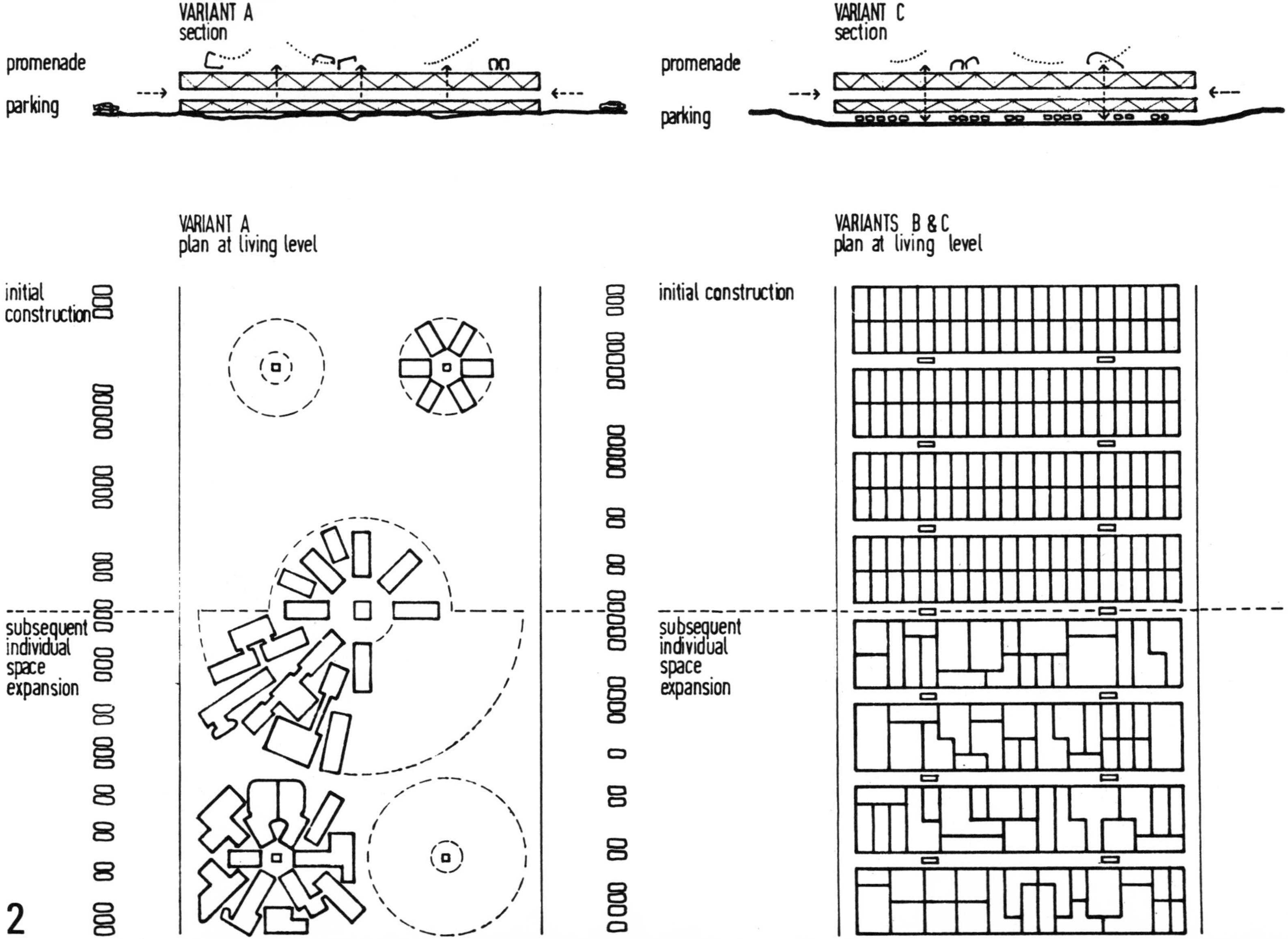

VARIANT A
section

promenade

parking

VARIANT C
section

promenade

parking

VARIANT A
plan at living level

initial construction

subsequent individual space expansion

VARIANTS B & C
plan at living level

initial construction

subsequent individual space expansion

2

70. *Michael Webb: A drive-in home within a megastructure serviced by electrical mobile containers, drawing, 1966. (A) Mobile unit. (B) Fixed floor space. (C) Bed unit. (D) Dressing area. (E) Bathroom. (G) Garden. (J) Study unit. (K) Kitchen.*

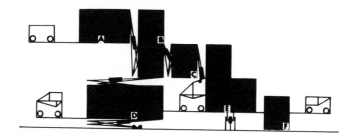

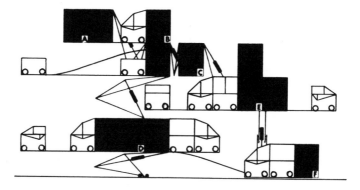

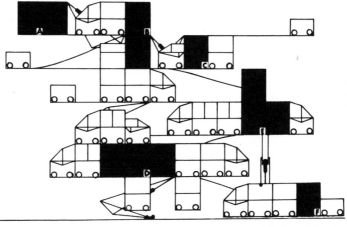

Michael Webb

71. *Michael Webb and David Greene: Drive-in Housing project showing service unit articulations, sections, 1966.*

In "A Home Is Not a House"[64] (1965), Reyner Banham, like Michael Webb and David Greene, starts from an intensely motorized community living in homes which have elaborate mechanical and electrical services built into them. (Banham's piece is addressed to the American scene, where individuals are more mechanically mobile and dwellings more completely serviced than anywhere else.) On the assumption that it is not the castle character of the dwelling that people are addicted to (as the increasing popularity of trailer homes testifies), but rather the comfort standards produced by new, better, and more efficient servicing, Banham makes his proposition: If twentieth-century resources and resourcefulness were to concentrate upon the design of a transportable "standard-of-living package" (i.e., a unit providing a capacity for all habitation service needs—heating, cooling, cooking, lighting, drainage, air control, power, etc.—to be contained within a portable, inflatable envelope, and capable of being moved, as and when desired), would this not provide a new potential in "no-houses" to end all houses (*Fig. 72*)?

David Greene and Michael Webb in pursuing the concept that a house is perhaps only a skin to live within, but one that is mobile, have produced two living units at different scales, the Living Pod (1966) and the Cushicle (1966).[65] David Greene's Living Pod is a two-story fiberglass mobile home with retractable legs (or wheels), in which the servicing tubes are separated from the shell and can be located as required (*Figs. 73–75*). Michael Webb's Cushicle is an idea for a mechanized mobile individual living unit consisting of a tubular chassis which can be propelled (floating on an air cushion), and a two-layer clothing skin, which in combination with the chassis can be inflated to make a chaise longue, or further inflated to make a room (*Fig. 76*).

Information Transfer

The new problem situation of architecture (i.e., that area of constantly changing concern characterized by the new questions which arise) contains a comparatively sophisticated interest in matters of physical movement and transportation, but the idea of an information movement which has, among other things, a complementary effect on physical movement, is only beginning to evolve as one of the new major issues.

It is now ninety years since the telephone came into public use, and over this time telephone channel transmission has extensively affected human behavior and patterns of physical location, although its influence has been largely passive rather than manipulated. (Marshall McLuhan has noted that the telephone has been responsible for the elimination of the red-light district and the creation of the call girl.)[66] But only comparatively recently has the problem of trying

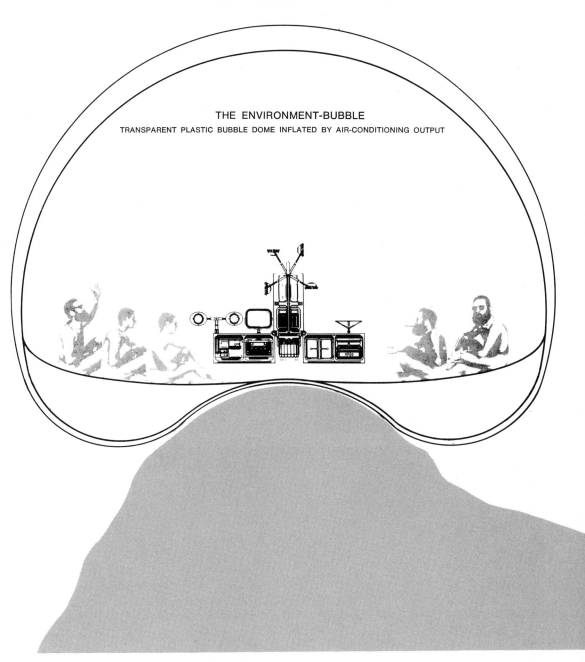

72. *Reyner Banham: The standard-of-living package in plastic dome inflated by conditioned air blown out by the package itself, 1965.*

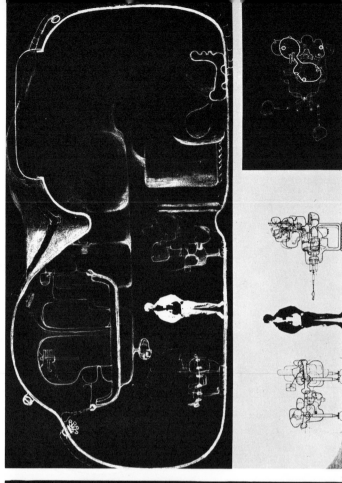

74. *Living Pod, photo diagrams.*

73. *David Greene: Living Pod, a fully applianced house, model, 1966.*

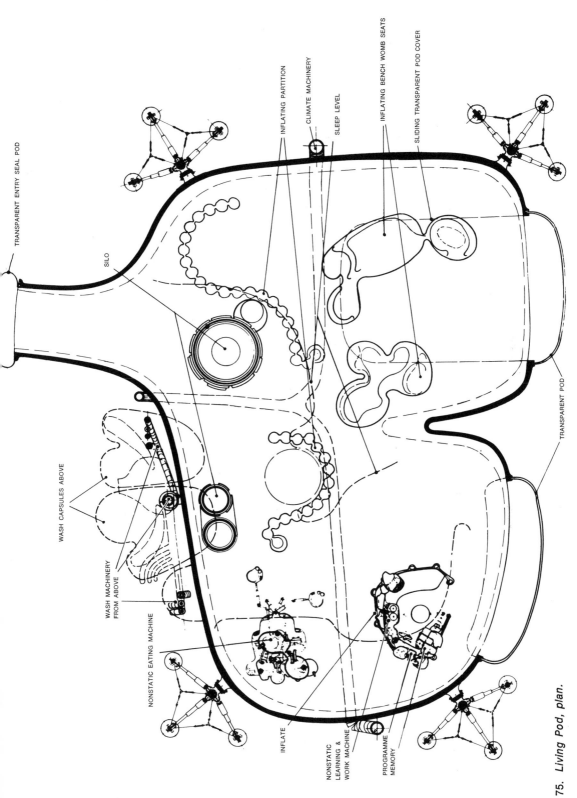

TRANSPARENT ENTRY SEAL POD

INFLATING PARTITION

CLIMATE MACHINERY

SLEEP LEVEL

INFLATING BENCH WOMB SEATS

SLIDING TRANSPARENT POD COVER

SILO

TRANSPARENT POD

WASH CAPSULES ABOVE

WASH MACHINERY FROM ABOVE

NONSTATIC EATING MACHINE

INFLATE

NONSTATIC LEARNING & WORK MACHINE

PROGRAMME MEMORY

75. *Living Pod, plan.*

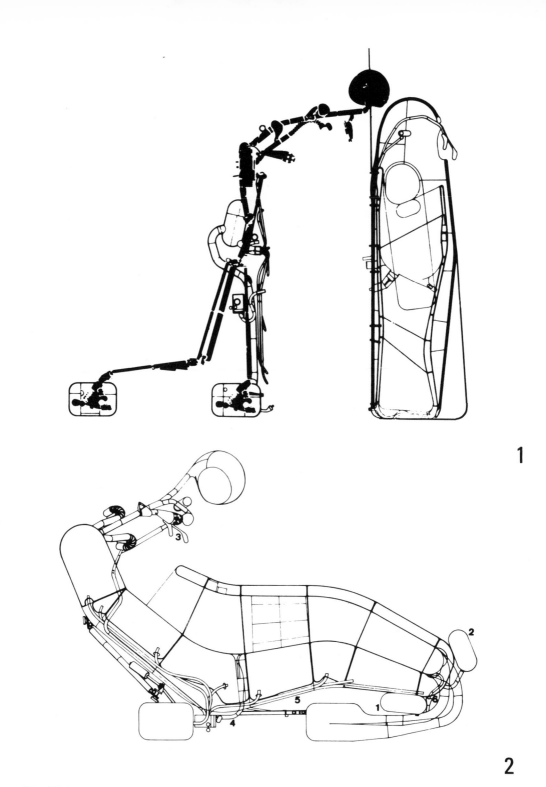

1

2

76. *Michael Webb: Cushicle, diagrams, 1966. (1) The Cushicle and the suit. (2) The Cushicle and suit as a chaise longue. (3) The room.*

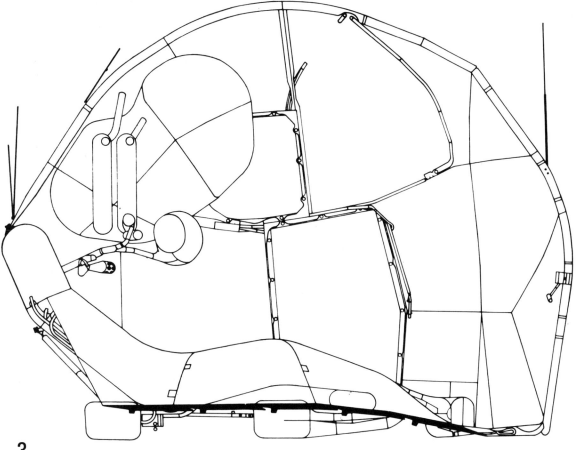

3

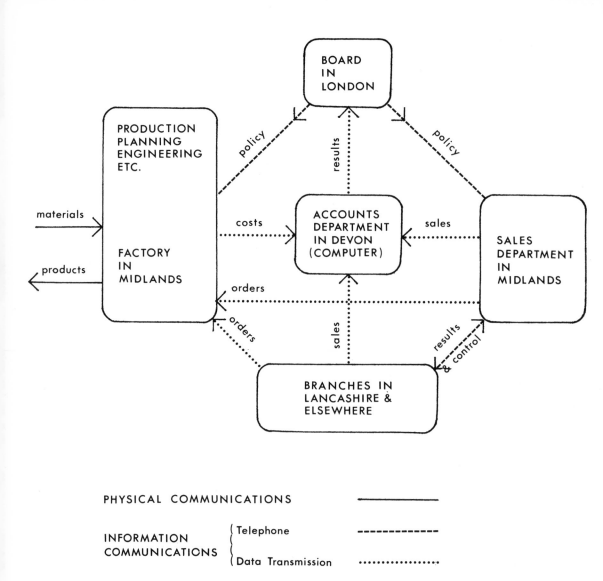

77. *John Harper: Communication requirements of an imaginary firm, diagram,*
1965.

to understand the information network become a matter of critical theoretical study, as, for example, in Peter Cowan's new program on Urban Information Systems[67] which has developed out of an earlier study of the office building phenomenon (and which is primarily an information processing machine).

The decentralization of commerce from city centers, and the outward movement of city dwellers into lower density suburban and rural areas, has been both encouraged and facilitated by the availability of information transfer services. John Harper's hypothetical model on the communicational requirements for a business[68] (*Fig. 77*) illustrates a network which decentralizes from the city all commercial operations except those of the governing board of directors, and demonstrates, in a more general way, a possible subdivisibility of operations in terms which distinguish the needs of physical movement from those of information movement.

Development in communication channel technology, and in hardware for information storage and retrieval, is increasingly affecting the form and the potential of existing information institutions and is providing the opportunity for new concepts which could exploit the new capacities. Data storage banks, video tapes, films, or microslides, instantaneously retrievable or transmittable through visual or aural mechanisms, are giving information institutions such as libraries and educational facilities a new dimension which the architect is having to accommodate in an unrestrictive way.

The Education Department of the Corporation of Glasgow, in December, 1963, began the first closed-circuit television education program in Britain, linking up three hundred schools. Other programs followed, including experiments by the Department of Education and Science (*Fig. 78*) and the Inner London Education Authority.

78. *Department of Education and Science: The Oastler College, Huddersfield (Teachers' Training College). View of classroom in closed-circuit television system study, 1963.*

Open transmission sound and television educational programs are now extensively used in homes and schools, but the educational enterprise which could have a major effect on the future of many areas of learning, as well as upon the future physical nature of higher education establishments, is the University of the Air[69] project, now called the Open University, and being developed by the Department of Education and Science. In this, courses will be offered and degrees will be earned—in the living room.

A scheme almost exclusively addressed to the potentials of information transfer is the O.C.H.[70] feasibility study by Cedric Price (1966) (*Fig. 79*), applied to an existing site in the center of London (the junction of Tottenham Court Road and Oxford Street), for a national catering organization client, J. Lyons & Co. O.C.H. is at a walk-through location, and offers the Central London public an information machine for up to 5,000 people, to contain extensive telecommunicational facilities and information storage equipment. O.C.H. can be used as a citizens' inquiry service where teleconnections can be made to press news rooms, travel agencies, government ministries, to Parliament, industry, commerce, etc., thus making information accessible which is at present under-used or ignored because of access difficulties (*Fig. 80A*). Or, O.C.H. can offer a skill-learning or research facility service through programed machines (a Link drive-a-car trainer or a language-teaching machine) or through teleconnections to other study centers (*Fig. 80B*). Or, O.C.H. can be used as a center equipped to provide facilities for information exchange, at a meeting level, at a "conference" level, or at an inter-city (concurrent exchange) conference level (*Fig. 80C*).

The basic user component in the center would be the two-seater information carrel (with a series of possible physical arrangements), but open floor space for observation, wandering, wondering, rest, and refreshment by mobile preparation units is fundamental to the full use of the center (*Fig. 80D*).

It is perhaps symbolic of a telecommunications era that the new, highest building in Britain (580 feet), completed in 1966, should be the London Post Office Tower, with its revolving restaurant, public observation galleries, and an aerial section for transmitting the microwave radio relay signals over the highest structures in the city (*Figs. 81–82*).

Matters of Complexity and Toward a Better Understanding

In this essay, I have attempted to give an indication of certain areas of the British architectural context and then to illustrate some ideas which are influencing present architectural thinking, ideas which are being talked about and experimented with. I have, however, considered technology primarily in terms of its availability to solve problems,

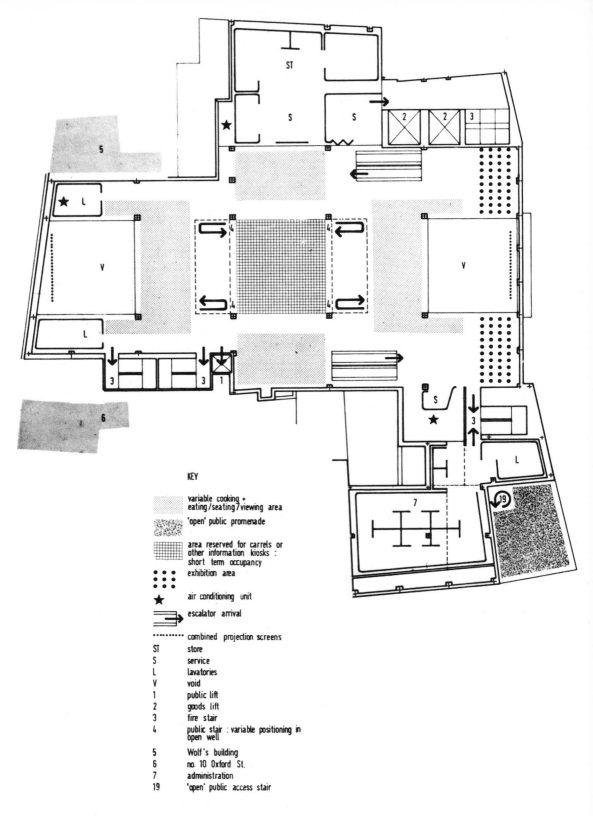

KEY

▓ variable cooking +
eating/seating/viewing area

▒ 'open' public promenade

▦ area reserved for carrels or
other information kiosks :
short term occupancy

••• exhibition area
•••

★ air conditioning unit

▤→ escalator arrival

·········· combined projection screens

ST   store
S   service
L   lavatories
V   void
1   public lift
2   goods lift
3   fire stair
4   public stair : variable positioning in
      open well

5   Wolf's building
6   no. 10 Oxford St.
7   administration
19   'open' public access stair

79. *Cedric Price: O.C.H., plan of second floor, 1966.*

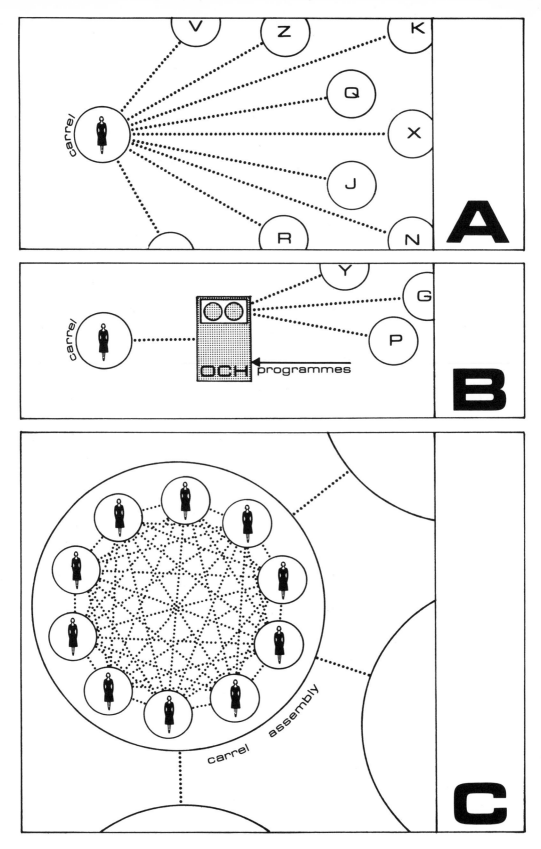

80. *O.C.H., diagrams of four of the communications facilities.*

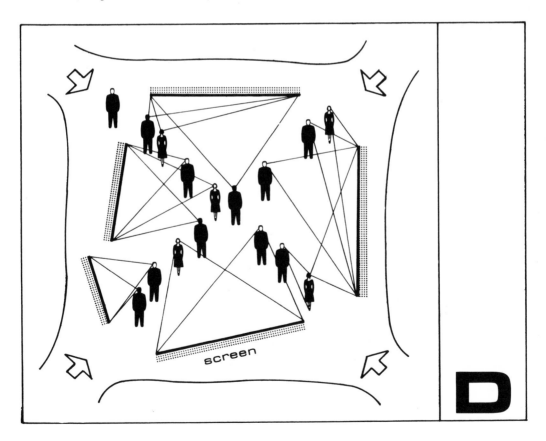

81. *Ministry of Public Building and Works Architect's Department: Post Office Tower, London, 1966.*

82. *Post Office Tower, section.*

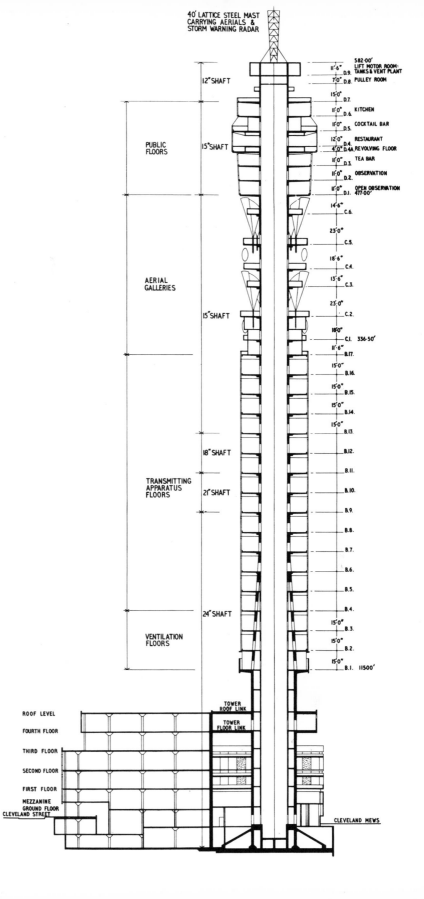

40' LATTICE STEEL MAST
CARRYING AERIALS &
STORM WARNING RADAR

		582·00'
11'·6"	D.9.	LIFT MOTOR ROOM: TANKS & VENT PLANT
7'·0"	D.8.	PULLEY ROOM
12" SHAFT		
15'·0"	D.7.	
11'·0"	D.6.	KITCHEN
11'·0"	D.5.	COCKTAIL BAR
PUBLIC FLOORS	15" SHAFT	
12'·0"	D.4.	RESTAURANT
4'·0"	D.4A.	REVOLVING FLOOR
11'·0"	D.3.	TEA BAR
11'·0"	D.2.	OBSERVATION
11'·0"	D.1.	OPEN OBSERVATION 477·00'
14'·6"	C.6.	
23'·0"	C.5.	
18'·6"	C.4.	
AERIAL GALLERIES	13'·6"	C.3.
15" SHAFT	23'·0"	C.2.
18'·0"	C.1.	336·50'
11'·6"	B.17.	
15'·0"	B.16.	
15'·0"	B.15.	
15'·0"	B.14.	
15'·0"	B.13.	
18" SHAFT		B.12.
		B.11.
TRANSMITTING APPARATUS FLOORS	21" SHAFT	B.10.
		B.9.
		B.8.
		B.7.
		B.6.
		B.5.
		B.4.
24" SHAFT		
15'·0"	B.3.	
VENTILATION FLOORS	15'·0"	B.2.
15'·0"	B.1.	115·00'

ROOF LEVEL

FOURTH FLOOR

THIRD FLOOR

SECOND FLOOR

FIRST FLOOR

MEZZANINE
GROUND FLOOR
CLEVELAND STREET

TOWER
ROOF LINK

TOWER
FLOOR LINK

CLEVELAND MEWS

while not intending to deny that new technological developments generate their own possibilities, as, for example, in the recent advances in pneumatic structures[71] which have made this topic a live issue in the current problem situation. Although part of a larger spectrum of studies, the development work on small electric vehicles, such as Eric Roberts' Town Sedan[72] (*Fig. 83*), is another live issue interesting architects because of its special relevance to possible new living patterns, as illustrated earlier by Michael Webb's Drive-in Housing.

But the increasing complexities in the British architectural scene since World War II have encouraged new ways of understanding it, and this has been one of the factors influencing a general shift of view in the direction of a more theory-oriented approach.

Perhaps the single most important factor in the change has been the computer, which offers its services for the solution of any question which can be characterized in a suitably quantified way. Even if the psychological optimism encouraged by the computer might be distinguished from its current mathematical possibilities, it has, nevertheless, been responsible for an increasingly "scientific" attitude (sometimes pseudo-scientific) which finds dissatisfaction in arbitrariness, and this approach has been responsible for certain new complementary developments.

One developing study has been that of design methodology. Work upon this subject has begun to reveal its many complexities.

83. *Eric J. Roberts and Associates: Town sedan or minimal car, drawings, 1965.*

Studies of problem structures have produced sophisticated analytical testing procedures,[73] but they have also shown that there are difficulties in accounting for the problem of invention in a satisfactory way.[74] In design, "doing" is simpler than "accounting for" (Gilbert Ryle's "knowing how" as distinguished from "knowing that").[75] Present modest computer aids in architectural practices, including programs for cost control (CBC),[76] structural analyses, user-requirement studies, and administrative control, are becoming common. But systematization, as a total view as much as a method, is being increasingly used in central and local government agency studies, in university research groups, and in private practice. In 1965, one third of all the schools completed in England[77] for that year were produced by "Consortia" of local authorities (of which there are eight) who work within the constraints of their systematized programs and employ system-building methods.

These sorts of examples are symptomatic of a shifting (if not shifted) viewpoint. By this view, architecture is not a discrete activity. A project, whether large or small, must be seen in its context as a component which has a relationship to other parts of its system. The certainty which was a part of the classically discrete program has moved towards a fluid but calculated uncertainty.

So if architecture is becoming mathematical at one level and anti-building at another, perhaps it *should* be classified as not architecture . . . but this *would* signify that it had taken a New Direction.

NOTES

1. K. R. Popper, "On the Sources of Knowledge and of Ignorance," *Conjectures and Refutations* (London: Routledge and Kegan Paul, 1963; New York: Basic Books, 1963).
2. I. Lakatos, "Infinite Regress and the Foundations of Mathematics," *The Aristotelian Society Supplementary Volume* XXXVI, London. (To be published in Proofs & Refutations, Cambridge University Press, 1969.)
3. F. A. Hayek, "The Dilemma of Specialization," *Studies in Philosophy, Politics and Economics* (London: Routledge and Kegan Paul, 1967; Chicago: The University of Chicago Press, 1967).
4. *Ibid.*, p. 124.
5. N. Wiener, *The Human Use of Human Beings* (Boston: Houghton Mifflin Company, 1950).
6. Thomas S. Kuhn, *The Structure of Scientific Revolutions* (Chicago: The University of Chicago Press, 1962).
7. J. C. W. Reith, *Into the Wind* (London: Hodder & Stoughton, 1949).
8. *Report of the Royal Commission on Distribution of Industrial Population* (London: H.M.S.O., 1940). (Barlow Report.)
9. *Expert Committee on Compensation and Betterment. Final Report* (London: H.M.S.O., 1942). (Uthwatt Report.)
   Committee on Utilization of Land in Rural Areas. Report. (London: H.M.S.O., 1942). (Scott Report.)
10. Patrick Abercrombie and J. H. Forshaw, *County of London Plan* (London: Macmillan, 1943).
    Patrick Abercrombie, *Greater London Plan, 1944* (London: H.M.S.O., 1945).
11. Abercrombie, *Greater London Plan*, p. 22.
12. Ebenezer Howard, *To-morrow: A Peaceful Path to Real Reform*, 1898. Second edition renamed *Garden Cities of To-morrow* (1902).
13. Jane Jacobs, *The Death and Life of Great American Cities* (New York: Random House, 1962; London: Jonathan Cape, 1962).
14. Ebenezer Howard, *Garden Cities of To-morrow* (London: Faber and Faber, 1946).
15. New Towns were usually built around small existing village cores, but in Welwyn Garden City the population by 1948 was only 18,500 (Howard's plan had been for a town of 50,000), so the New Town legislation was used as a means of developing the town further.
16. For a detailed account of the composition of the New Towns, see Osborn and Whittick, *The New Towns* (London: Leonard Hill, 1963); see also Lloyd Rodwin, *The British New Towns Policy* (Cambridge: Harvard University Press, 1956).
17. Lewis Mumford, "Old Forms for New Towns," *The Highway and the City* (New York: Mentor Edition, 1964).
18. J. M. Richards, "The Failure of New Towns," *Architectural Review* (London), July, 1953.
19. *Ibid.*, p. 31.

20. Reyner Banham, *The New Brutalism* (London: Architectural Press, 1966; New York: Reinhold Publishing Corporation, 1966), p. 12.
21. See Ministry of Health and Ministry of Works, *Housing Manual 1944* (London: H.M.S.O.); Ministry of Health, *Housing Manual 1949* (London: H.M.S.O.); Ministry of Works and Ministry of Local Government and Planning, *Housing Manual, 1949* (London: H.M.S.O.).
22. Gloag and Wornum, *House out of Factory* (London: George Allen and Unwin, 1946). An early "popularizing" book on prefabrication.
23. See Reyner Banham, *op cit.*, and Robin Middleton, "The New Brutalism or a clean, well lighted place," *Architectural Design* (London), January, 1967.
24. A program known as the "Lessor" scheme.
25. The Building By-Laws had originally been drawn up around the requirements of Victorian-Georgian buildings. Rules were laid down, for example, on areas of walls relative to areas of windows, heights of window heads, etc. It was less troublesome and less time-wasting to conform with the by-laws than to appeal for permission to deviate.
26. R. B. White, *Prefabrication: A History of its Development in Great Britain* (London: H.M.S.O., 1965).
27. Patrick Abercrombie, *Town and Country Planning* (London: Oxford University Press, 1933), p. 117.
28. *Ibid.*, p. 127.
29. For a discussion of the problems posed by Sociological Determinism in the sense that I mean here, see Maurice Broady, "Social Theory in Architectural Design," *Arena* (London), January, 1966.
30. Alison and Peter Smithson, *Urban Structuring* (London: Studio Vista, 1967).
31. Jack Lynn, "Park Hill Redevelopment, Sheffield," *RIBA Journal* (London), December, 1962.
32. Jack Lynn said that "the elevations were not 'composed' in the usual sense in fact were never drawn." *Ibid.*, p. 454.
33. Reyner Banham, *op cit.*, p. 87.
34. Out of a total of under 10,000. Source R.I.B.A. estimate derived from 1949 R.I.B.A. inquiry.
35. Out of a total of 17,500. Source R.I.B.A. sample survey, 1958.
36. Out of a total of 20,000. Source R.I.B.A. inquiry 1964. Fuller details show private practice 50 percent, public service 39 percent of which central government 7 percent, national boards 4 percent, local government including New Towns 28 percent, teaching 3 percent, other 8 percent.
37. Refer to Directorate of Economic Intelligence, *Annual Bulletin of Construction Statistics*, Ministry of Public Building and Works, London.
38. Ministry of Education, "Wokingham School Development Project," *Building Bulletin No. 8* (London: H.M.S.O., 1952). An interesting note on certain shortcomings of this report can be found in R. B. White, *Prefabrication* (London: H.M.S.O., 1965), p. 238.
39. Ministry of Education, "C.L.A.S.P.," *Building Bulletin No. 19* (London: H.M.S.O., 1961).
40. The structuring of work in both public and private architects' offices in Britain was examined in detail in the report of the R.I.B.A. Survey: *The Architect and his Office* (1962).
41. The Hills Presweld steel frames were usually clad externally with precast concrete slabs. Roof slabs were of precast concrete troughs spanning between roof beams at 8-foot 3-inch centers, cement screeded, and covered with roofing felt.

42. *Report of the Royal Commission on Local Government in Greater London* (London: H.M.S.O., 1960). (Herbert Commission.)
43. Edward Hollamby, "Housing in London," *RIBA Journal* (London), August, 1967.
44. J. W. Davidson, "S.F.I." *Architectural Design* (London), March, 1967, p. 138.
45. *The Planning of a New Town* (London: Greater London Council, 1965).
46. Ministry of Transport, *Traffic in Towns* (London: H.M.S.O., 1963). (Buchanan Report.)
47. See *A.A. Journal* (London), May, 1964. Refer "On Cities and Traffic" by Peter Hall, "On Traffic and Urban Design" by Colin Buchanan, and see comments by Cedric Price, p. 321.
48. Abercrombie, *Greater London Plan.*
49. Ministry of Housing and Local Government, *The South East Study, 1961–1981* (London: H.M.S.O., 1964).
50. The Department of Economic Affairs redefined the South East Region so that part of the area covered by the *South East Study* is now included in the East Anglia Region. The revised population growth for the new South East Region is predicted as over two million.
51. At the time of writing (April, 1968), the Southampton–Portsmouth City has not been given a start date.
52. Here are details of Mark III Cities giving name, date of designation, and projected 1981 populations: Central Lancashire, 1967, 500,000; Dawley-Wellington-Oakengates, 1966, 200,000; Northampton, 1966, 222,000; Ipswich, 1966, 219,000 Peterborough, 1966, 175,000; Warrington-Risley, 1967, 180,000; Milton Keynes, 1967, 121,000; Skelmersdale, 1961, 70,000; Runcorn, 1964, 77,000; Redditch, 1964, 73,000; Washington, 1964, 70,000.
53. Colin Buchanan & Partners in association with Economic Consultants Ltd., *South Hampshire Study* (London: H.M.S.O., 1966).
54. See Patrick Abercrombie's 1933 statement, ". . . urban and rural can never be interchangeable adjectives," *Town and Country Planning* (London: Oxford University Press, 1933).
55. Lionel March, "Homes beyond the fringe," *RIBA Journal* (London), August, 1967.
56. See "Archigram Group London: A chronological survey," *Architectural Design* (London), November, 1965.
57. Joan Littlewood, "A laboratory of fun," *New Scientist* (London), 14 May 1964, p. 432.
58. The Potteries Thinkbelt was a self-sponsored project designed during 1964 and 1965. See Cedric Price, "PTb," *Architectural Design* (London), October, 1966, and "Potteries Thinkbelt," *New Society* (London), 2 June 1966.
59. The Pottery Towns include Stoke-on-Trent, Hanley, and Burslem. Newcastle-under-Lyme is also within the Thinkbelt area.
60. "Potteries Thinkbelt," *New Society* (London), 2 June 1966.
61. Robert L. Drew, "Estuaries—for Use or Ornament?", *The Philosophical Journal*, Vol. 4, No. 1 (1967), pp. 51–64. See also Fred Cottrell, *Energy and Society* (New York: McGraw-Hill Book Company, 1955).
62. Robert L. Drew, "The Solway Project," *Journal of the Town Planning Institute* (London), March, 1965.
63. Michael Webb and David Greene, "Drive-in housing," *Architectural Design* (London), November, 1966.
64. Reyner Banham, "A Home Is Not a House," *Art in America* (New York), April, 1965.

65. See Michael Webb and David Greene, *op. cit.*

66. Marshall McLuhan *Understanding Media* (New York: McGraw-Hill Book Company, 1964).

67. This urban information study is being undertaken by the Joint Unit for Planning Research, London (University College and the London School of Economics). The study, "The Office—a facet of urban growth" (1967), has just been completed by this unit.

68. John Harper, "On Telecommunications," *A.A. Journal* (London), May, 1965.

69. See Department of Education and Science, *A University of the Air* (London: H.M.S.O., 1966), and *University of the Air: a Strathclyde view* (Glasgow: University of Strathclyde, 1965).

70. The project was named after its location, Oxford Street Corner House.

71. See *Proceedings of the 1st International Colloquium on Pneumatic Structures* (Stuttgart, Germany: University of Stuttgart, 1967).

72. Brian Richards, *New Movement in Cities* (London: Studio Vista, 1966).

73. J. Christopher Jones and D. G. Thornley (Eds.), *Conference on design methods* (Oxford: Pergamon Press, 1963), and S. A. Gregory (Ed.), *Design method* (London: Butterworth, 1966).

74. See author's "Towards a Structure for Architectural Ideas," *Arena* (London), June, 1965. Also see David Bohm, "On Creativity," *Arena* (London), May, 1967.

75. Gilbert Ryle, "Knowing How and Knowing That," *The Concept of Mind* (London: Hutchinson, 1949).

76. CBC is Co-ordinated Building Communication, a comprehensive system for coding, classification, and costing. See CBC Progress in *Architects' Journal* (London), 24 January, 31 January, 7 February 1968. The system was described in the *Architects' Journal* between 25 March 1964 and 6 October 1965 (19 issues).

77. G. H. Wigglesworth, "Schools Consortia and the future," *RIBA Journal* (London), June, 1966.

INDEX

Sources of Illustrations

Illustrations not acknowledged below are reproduced by kind permission of the architects and designers.

1. Map by Janet Landau, London.
2. Faber and Faber Ltd., London.
3–5. Maps by Janet Landau, London.
6. Greater London Council.
7. Aluminium Development Association, London.
8–9. Photograph, de Burgh Galwey; *Architectural Review*, London.
10. Photograph, Millar & Harris, London; *Architects' Journal*, London.
11. Photograph, de Burgh Galwey; *Architectural Review*, London.
14. Photograph, de Burgh Galwey; *Architectural Review*, London.
15. Photograph, Arthur Winter; *Architects' Journal*, London.
16. Drawing by Peter Sigmonde.
17. Photograph, Henry Snoek; *The Economist*, London.
18–19. Photographs, Michael Carapetian; Tehran, Iran.
20–21. Greater London Council.
22–23. Photographs, Wm. J. Toomey; *Architects' Journal*, London.
24. Photograph, John Donat, London.
25. Photograph, Sam Lambert; *Architectural Review*, London.
26–27. Ministry of Public Building and Works, London.
28–29. Greater London Council.
31–35. Greater London Council.
36–37. Photographs, the author.
38. Map by Janet Landau, London.
39. Photograph, Bryan and Shear; Cumbernauld Development Corporation, Scotland.
40. Map by Janet Landau, London.
41–42. Controller of H.M.S.O., London.
57. Map by Richard Natkiel, London.
61–62. National Tower Testing Station, Cheddar, Somerset.
63. Collage by Janet Landau, London.
67. Greater London Council.
68. Mickleover of London.
72. Drawing by François Dallegret, *Art in America* (New York), No. 2, 1965.
78. The Marconi Company Ltd., London.
80. Diagram by Janet Landau, London.
81–82. H. M. Postmaster General, London.